REFLECTIONS FOR **DAILY PRAYER**
TRINITY 13 TO **CHRIST THE KING**
18 AUGUST – 29 NOVEMBER 2008

JOHN PRITCHARD
JANE WILLIAMS
TOM SMAIL
EMMA INESON
MAGGI DAWN
ALAN GARROW
IAN PAUL

Church House Publishing
Church House
Great Smith Street
London SW1P 3AZ

Tel: 020 7898 1451
Fax: 020 7898 1449

ISBN 978 0 7151 4159 5

Published 2008 by Church House Publishing
Copyright © The Archbishops' Council 2008

All rights reserved. No part of this publication may be reproduced or stored or transmitted by any means or in any form, electronic or mechanical, including photocopying, recording, or any information storage and retrieval system, without written permission, which should be sought from the Copyright Administrator, Church House Publishing, Church House, Great Smith Street, London SW1P 3AZ.

Email: copyright@c-of-e.org.uk

The opinions expressed in this book are those of the authors and do not necessarily reflect the official policy of the General Synod or The Archbishops' Council of the Church of England.

Designed and typeset by Hugh Hillyard-Parker
Printed by Halstan & Co. Ltd, Amersham, Bucks

Contents

About the authors	vi
About *Reflections for Daily Prayer*	1
Monday 18 August to Saturday 30 August JOHN PRITCHARD	2
Monday 1 September to Wednesday 17 September JANE WILLIAMS	14
Thursday 18 September to Saturday 4 October TOM SMAIL	29
Monday 6 October to Saturday 18 October EMMA INESON	44
Monday 20 October to Saturday 1 November MAGGI DAWN	56
Monday 3 November to Saturday 15 November ALAN GARROW	68
Monday 17 November to Saturday 29 November IAN PAUL	80

About the authors

John Pritchard is Bishop of Oxford. He has been Director of Pastoral Studies at Cranmer Hall in St John's College Durham and subsequently Warden. He became Archdeacon of Canterbury and Canon Residentiary of Canterbury Cathedral in 1996 and Bishop of Jarrow in 2002. He is the author of several books on practical theology and aspects of Christian discipleship.

Jane Williams is a popular writer. She lectures at St Paul's Theological Centre and is a visiting lecturer at King's College London. She taught previously at Trinity Theological College, Bristol.

Tom Smail was Vice-Principal and Lecturer in Doctrine at St John's College, Nottingham from 1979 to 1984, and then led a church in Croydon until his retirement in 1994. He is an acclaimed speaker and continues to lecture and preach in the UK and abroad.

Emma Ineson is Tutor in Practical Theology at Trinity College, Bristol and also has responsibility for spirituality there. Before coming to Bristol she worked as a curate in Sheffield and then as Chaplain to the Lee Abbey Christian Community and Retreat Centre in Devon.

Maggi Dawn was ordained into the Anglican Church in 1999 after spending a number of years working as a singer, writer and musician in the field of contemporary music. Previously Chaplain at King's College, Cambridge, she became Chaplain at Robinson College, Cambridge, in September 2003. She is an occasional broadcaster for BBC Radio 4 Religion and is a regular speaker at Greenbelt Festival.

Alan Garrow is Vicar Theologian of Bath Abbey. He was previously Director of Studies on the Oxford and St Albans Ministry Course, where he taught New Testament. His publications include works on Matthew and Revelation.

Ian Paul is Dean of Studies at St John's College, Nottingham where he teaches New Testament and hermeneutics. Prior to moving to Nottingham he was in parish ministry for ten years in Poole, Dorset. He is Managing Editor of Grove Books Ltd and a member of General Synod.

About *Reflections for Daily Prayer*

Based on the *Common Worship Lectionary* readings for Morning Prayer, these daily reflections are designed to refresh and inspire times of personal prayer. The aim is to provide rich, contemporary and engaging insights into Scripture.

Each page lists the lectionary readings for the day, with the main psalms for that day highlighted in **bold**. The Collect of the day – either the *Common Worship* collect or the shorter additional collect – is also included.

For those using this book in conjunction with a service of Morning Prayer, the following conventions apply: a psalm printed in parentheses is omitted if it has been used as the opening canticle at that office; a psalm marked with an asterisk may be shortened if desired.

A short reflection is provided on either the Old or New Testament reading. Popular writers, experienced ministers, biblical scholars and theologians will be contributing to this series. They all bring their own emphases, enthusiasms and approaches to biblical interpretation to bear.

Regular users of Morning Prayer and *Time to Pray* (from *Common Worship: Daily Prayer*) and anyone who follows the lectionary for their regular Bible reading will benefit from the rich variety of traditions represented in these stimulating and accessible pieces.

Ordinary Time

Monday 18 August

Psalms 123, 124, 125, **126**
2 Samuel 18.1-18
Acts 10.34-end

Acts 10.34-end

I have long suspected that God is not as tidy as I am. God's ways seem at times to be quite careless of our well-crafted systems of belief and practice. Here in Caesarea, God decides to pour out the gift of the Holy Spirit on a group of 'Johnny-come-latelys' who haven't even been circumcised, let alone baptized. It's a scandal.

Peter had been doing his bit. He came to Caesarea under the compulsion of a dream and proceeded to do what any good apostle would do – he reminded them of the story of Jesus from arrival to departure. However, the Spirit interrupted, as he often does. 'While Peter was still speaking', the Holy Spirit 'fell' (not just 'alighted gently'), and all heaven broke loose. All Peter could do was to try to regularize what God was doing and to baptize the group forthwith.

There's always a danger that we Christians will try to make systems out of the reckless freedom of God, and that we'll try to make God manageable and the Church tidy. A rather more faithful strategy is to watch closely for what God is doing and to respond gratefully. We'll find ourselves in strange company and in edgy situations, but it makes the Christian life much more exciting.

COLLECT

Almighty God,
who called your Church to bear witness
that you were in Christ reconciling the world to yourself:
help us to proclaim the good news of your love,
that all who hear it may be drawn to you;
through him who was lifted up on the cross,
and reigns with you in the unity of the Holy Spirit,
one God, now and for ever.

Ordinary Time

Psalms **132**, 133
2 Samuel 18.19 – 19.8a
Acts 11.1-18

Tuesday 19 August

Acts 11.1-18

It's all very well going freelance and changing the rules, but the time comes when you have to go to the rulemakers and justify your outrageous behaviour. Peter had to go to Jerusalem and explain why he had baptized outsiders (Gentiles). The importance that Luke attaches to the story is demonstrated by the fact that he has Peter repeating it yet again.

The reception may not have been particularly hostile – the early Church was used to being led forward by the Spirit – but it was nevertheless a defining moment for the young Church, and the response is awed silence. The apostles and believers knew they were being addressed by God. When God acts in a decisive way, it doesn't leave much room for group discussion.

The trick is to recognize what is an act of God and what's a hare-brained idea from the back row of the PCC. Discernment in this kind of situation is an art that comes through a mature mix of steady prayer, corporate reflection and holy instinct. It's a heavy responsibility on the leadership of churches, but one thing is clear: no one wants to be in the position of 'hindering God' (v.17). Today's Church has a special need to be brave. Guarding our backs isn't sufficient. We might be left behind.

Almighty God,
you search us and know us:
may we rely on you in strength
and rest on you in weakness,
now and in all our days;
through Jesus Christ our Lord.

COLLECT

Ordinary Time

Wednesday 20 August

Psalm 119.153-end
2 Samuel 19.8b-23
Acts 11.19-end

Acts 11.19-end

The genie was out of the bottle. Gentiles were now going to find Christ in all sorts of places, starting with Antioch. The Jerusalem believers sent Special Investigator Barnabas to see what was going on, and they couldn't have made a better choice. Wherever you meet Barnabas in Acts, he's encouraging, supporting, affirming, pioneering.

In today's passage, Barnabas encourages the vibrant new church in Antioch, offers the newly discovered evangelist Saul his first big break, and takes much-needed relief-funding to believers in Judea. He was recognized as having the wonderful cocktail of being 'a good man, full of the Holy Spirit and of faith' (v.24). How we might wish for the same qualities!

The impression you get is of a man who lived so close to his Lord that his Christlikeness was recognized by all. His most noticeable quality is of encouragement – hence his name, which means (roughly) 'son of encouragement'. It's a good discipline to try to live a whole day, or week, with that same filter of encouragement on everything we say in our relationships and encounters. There aren't many conversations where it's impossible. Under encouragement, people grow, smile and become creative; we ourselves feel better about life; and the kingdom is advanced. It's a classic win–win–win.

COLLECT

Almighty God,
who called your Church to bear witness
that you were in Christ reconciling the world to yourself:
help us to proclaim the good news of your love,
that all who hear it may be drawn to you;
through him who was lifted up on the cross,
and reigns with you in the unity of the Holy Spirit,
one God, now and for ever.

Ordinary Time

Psalms **143**, 146
2 Samuel 19.24-end
Acts 12.1-17

Thursday 21 August

Acts 12.1-17

Apart from his presence at the Council of Jerusalem in Acts 15, this is Peter's last appearance in Luke's narrative. He hadn't planned the prison break, and the believers were praying, not plotting. The story is full of dramatic realism, even down to the detail of the maid, Rhoda, being so flustered that she left Peter at the door rather than letting him in.

The notion of angelic intervention in the affairs of humans had evolved since the Exile and would be relatively unchallenged. What we make of it now is up to us. An experienced priest was fond of saying: 'Experience is sacred; interpretation is free.' But what all of us can take away is the confidence that God constantly works for our rescue and restitution, and uses as many means as are available. Divine messengers appear in many forms, most of them human, as our friends (and others who surprise us) turn up at our door in time of need.

Once we have recognized that life is not hostile to us, but infused with a loving purpose, we are able hopefully to trust ourselves to God more generously – and perhaps also to be an 'angelic presence' to other people who find themselves living in life's many hard prisons.

COLLECT

Almighty God,
you search us and know us:
may we rely on you in strength
and rest on you in weakness,
now and in all our days;
through Jesus Christ our Lord.

Ordinary Time

Friday 22 August

Psalms 142, **144**
2 Samuel 23.1-7
Acts 12.18-end

Acts 12.18-end

Herod Agrippa was the grandson of Herod the Great, the Herod who was involved in the stories of Jesus' birth – and the bad genes seem to have passed to him with no trouble at all. He callously puts to death the guards who had failed to keep track of Peter, and he gets angry with the people of Tyre and Sidon, probably over some economic matter. Luke clearly believes that his death from a bad stomach condition is a punishment by God for blasphemy (v.23).

The simple causal link between bad actions and bad health is not a belief Jesus subscribed to, as he demonstrated in his comments on those killed when the Tower of Siloam collapsed (Luke 13.4). Nevertheless, he knew that we live in a moral universe where actions have consequences, as is perfectly obvious today in the arena of family relationships or global carbon emissions. Whether it be in this world or in eternity, God's justice is a constant.

But even the slings and arrows of outrageous people can't hold back the advance of the word of God (v.24). In the contested environment of contemporary Western secular culture, it's a comfort to know that the kingdom of God is unstoppable, whatever neglect, nastiness or downright evil we do. We mustn't trade on God's graceful victory, but we can at least rely on it.

COLLECT

Almighty God,
who called your Church to bear witness
that you were in Christ reconciling the world to yourself:
help us to proclaim the good news of your love,
that all who hear it may be drawn to you;
through him who was lifted up on the cross,
and reigns with you in the unity of the Holy Spirit,
one God, now and for ever.

Ordinary Time

Psalm **147**
2 Samuel 24
Acts 13.1-12

Saturday 23 August

Acts 13.1-12

Antioch is now the new centre of the Church, and it is from here that its mission now radiates. The sending out of Saul and Barnabas is another defining moment for the young Church, arising as ever out of prayer (v.2). Their first destination is Cyprus, and Luke shows us immediately that the mission imperative will always be opposed. In this case, it's by a Jewish magician (the same word is used for the wise men in Luke 2.1).

Saul ('also known as Paul', v.9) denounces Elymas fiercely with a vehemence that might surprise the first-time reader: 'You son of the devil, you enemy of all righteousness...' (v.10). He also condemns Elymas to temporary blindness, knowing full well himself how disabling that can be. What we begin to see is the mounting conflict between Judaism and the Church that runs throughout the rest of Acts.

The lasting issue for contemporary Christians to chew over is how we deal with opposition. We generally assume that we need to employ the grace, love and patience that we see in Jesus – and that's absolutely right. However, there are also times when evil requires nothing less than uncompromising rejection. Other cultures experience more of this than the West, but we, in softer contexts, need to be aware of our tendency to compromise and fudge in the interest of good manners. Paul may have been over-robust at times; we might not be robust enough.

> Almighty God,
> you search us and know us:
> may we rely on you in strength
> and rest on you in weakness,
> now and in all our days;
> through Jesus Christ our Lord.

COLLECT

Ordinary Time

Monday 25 August

Psalms 1, 2, 3
1 Kings 1.5-31
Acts 13.13-43

1 Kings 1.5-31

It's the end of an era. 1 and 2 Kings chart the story of how the rich, extensive kingdom handed over by David gradually declined to its final destruction. Today's passage is just the start, but it demonstrates the danger of inadequate succession planning. Adonijah thought he could take over the throne by a pre-emptive strike, whereas Bathsheba is determined that Solomon shall have it. David confirms his promise that Solomon is his chosen heir, which leaves Adonijah somewhat exposed. His death is only one chapter away.

Politicians also know how difficult it is to hand over power cleanly, but the whiff of power makes fools of many. They scramble to fill the top spot, often feigning innocence. At least Adonijah was transparently ambitious. Paul's advice to the Romans seems wise: 'Do not think of yourselves more highly than you ought to think …' (Romans 12.3). If we submit ourselves to the just and gentle rule of Christ, unseemly ambition is dispersed, and (theoretically, at least) we seek only to be available to him for his purposes. As the Methodist Covenant puts it: 'Let me be employed for you or laid aside for you; exalted for you or brought low for you.'

Adonijah doesn't seem to have got the message, and sadly he will pay with his life.

COLLECT

Almighty God,
whose only Son has opened for us
a new and living way into your presence:
give us pure hearts and steadfast wills
to worship you in spirit and in truth;
through Jesus Christ your Son our Lord,
who is alive and reigns with you,
in the unity of the Holy Spirit,
one God, now and for ever.

Ordinary Time

Psalms **5**, 6, (8)
1 Kings 1.32 – 2.4,10-12
Acts 13.44 – 14.7

Tuesday 26 August

1 Kings 1.32 – 2.4,10-12

It's worth listening to the final words of a great leader. David hadn't got everything right, as the episode with Bathsheba demonstrated, but his heart had been fixed on serving God, and God had honoured that faithfulness. He passes on his 'life-principle' to Solomon: 'Be strong, be courageous, and keep the charge of the Lord your God, walking in his ways … so that you may prosper in all that you do' (2.2-3).

It sounds so simple. Just keep in step with the Lord, and everything will be fine. Unfortunately, it's both profoundly simple and profoundly complex. Although he was famously wise in many ways, Solomon found that it was also very difficult to keep the singleness of vision that was his father's trump card. Influenced by his many wives and concubines (1,000 according to 1 Kings 11.3!), he compromised on the worship of other gods, thus opening the door to the fatal subversion that was to destroy David's kingdom.

Keeping David's 'life-principle' of faithfulness is a daily decision for any believer. The siren voices will never go away; only a daily choice can sustain the commitment. But coming to meet us in our daily decision is an equal gift – God's grace is only a prayer away.

COLLECT

Merciful God,
your Son came to save us
and bore our sins on the cross:
may we trust in your mercy
and know your love,
rejoicing in the righteousness
that is ours through Jesus Christ our Lord.

Ordinary Time

Wednesday 27 August

Psalm **119.1-32**
1 Kings 3
Acts 14.8-end

1 Kings 3

Solomon got away to a fast start. He married sensibly (securing peace on his southern border); he made good appointments; and he started building the temple that his father had never quite managed. He had a bit of a dip by sacrificing to local deities (3.3), but he got top marks when the Lord offered him whatever he wanted and he asked for wisdom – 'an understanding mind ... able to discern between good and evil' (3.9) – rather than wealth or long life. He then proceeded to demonstrate that wisdom in the strange case of the two prostitutes and the disputed maternity of the surviving child.

What Solomon realized is that wisdom is priceless. It helped, of course, that because he'd answered the question well, God then gave him as much wealth as he could cope with. Nevertheless, he knew that he couldn't hope to hold down his job without the gift of wisdom. If only we could all make a similar choice and realize that 'all that glisters is not gold'. Greater wealth simply doesn't give greater happiness: it's proven both by research and by hard personal experience.

Real gold lies in recognizing that every day we will be faced with both good and evil – and having the wisdom to know the difference.

COLLECT

Almighty God,
whose only Son has opened for us
a new and living way into your presence:
give us pure hearts and steadfast wills
to worship you in spirit and in truth;
through Jesus Christ your Son our Lord,
who is alive and reigns with you,
in the unity of the Holy Spirit,
one God, now and for ever.

Ordinary Time

Psalms 14, **15**, 16
1 Kings 4.29 – 5.12
Acts 15.1-21

Thursday 28 August

1 Kings 4.29 – 5.12

'What's the big idea?', we sometimes ask, challengingly. Solomon's 'big idea' was to build the temple that David's years of warfare had made impracticable. It was a grandiose plan, to build a house of prayer in which the eternal, unlimited God would, in a sense, be 'localized' and available to his people. It was to be 'a house for the name of the Lord my God' (v.5), 'name' meaning much more than the word does to us today – more like 'God's whole personality'.

But to achieve this ambitious plan, Solomon had to employ his wisdom again in setting up a deal of mutual benefit with Hiram, the king who had the trees Solomon needed. It was an offer Hiram couldn't refuse, but it gave him both peace and prosperity for many years, and everyone emerged a winner. What made Solomon so effective at this stage in his kingship was his combination of high vision and close detail. He knew precisely what he was offering Hiram, but he also knew why he was offering it. He didn't lose the vision of a temple worthy of the Lord his God.

Leadership at any level – church, family, workplace – needs a similar combination of vision and practical detail, not just head in the clouds, nor just feet set in concrete. Having both skills may not come naturally – but God is a good teacher. Just ask.

COLLECT

Merciful God,
your Son came to save us
and bore our sins on the cross:
may we trust in your mercy
and know your love,
rejoicing in the righteousness
that is ours through Jesus Christ our Lord.

Ordinary Time

Friday 29 August

Psalms 17, **19**
1 Kings 6.1,11-28
Acts 15.22-35

1 Kings 6.1,11-28

The description of the construction of the temple in these chapters is the most detailed specification we have of a religious building in the ancient world. It was fairly modest in scale, the main hall being some 30 metres by 10, and the inner sanctuary 10 by 10. However, it was clearly of paramount importance for Israel, the focus of their devotion and their longing. Solomon spared no expense either; he covered many parts with gold.

We need focal places for our worship and prayers, and the people of God are tenacious in their attachment to their churches, the places that carry their memories and dreams, and that remind them of realities beyond the here and now. As we repair, re-order and beautify them, the dilemma is always present – is it right to spend so much money and energy on buildings, when the mission of the Church is with people?

There is no simple formula to answer that question, but we need to respect the deep instinct that wants to make places of beauty for a beautiful God, that wants to offer the very best we have to God, and that needs to come to places where 'prayer is valid' (T. S. Eliot). The human spirit would be terribly impoverished if we only had utilitarian buildings in which to touch the edge of the divine presence. Nevertheless, the question must always be asked, not least because it's probably God who is asking it.

COLLECT

Almighty God,
whose only Son has opened for us
a new and living way into your presence:
give us pure hearts and steadfast wills
to worship you in spirit and in truth;
through Jesus Christ your Son our Lord,
who is alive and reigns with you,
in the unity of the Holy Spirit,
one God, now and for ever.

Ordinary Time

Psalms 20, 21, **23**
1 Kings 8.1-30
Acts 15.36 – 16.5

Saturday 30 August

1 Kings 8.1-30

This was one of the great days of Israel's life. The Ark of the Covenant, that vital symbol of national identity and unity, is brought up the hill from the city of David and placed with great solemnity in the inner sanctuary. Solomon rises to the occasion with a prayer of dedication that praises God for his faithfulness to his promise (v.24) while at the same time recognizing that Israel has a matching responsibility to remain faithful to God. (The seeds of tragedy are already being planted.)

Solomon poses the problem that afflicts all shrines: 'But will God indeed dwell on the earth?' (v.27). How can you place infinity in a pint pot? The answer is that the temple is not meant to limit the infinite God, but it does allow faithful people to pray in or towards a place of supreme significance, while God is still 'in heaven your dwelling place' (v.30).

God gives us many aids and artefacts for our Christian journey – special places, special people, forms of worship, books and practices of prayer. These are wonderful gifts in the toolbag of discipleship, but they are clunky and inflexible tools at best. We do well to remember that everything is provisional, apart from God.

COLLECT

Merciful God,
your Son came to save us
and bore our sins on the cross:
may we trust in your mercy
and know your love,
rejoicing in the righteousness
that is ours through Jesus Christ our Lord.

Ordinary Time

Monday 1 September

Psalms 27, **30**
1 Kings 8.31-62
Acts 16.6-24

1 Kings 8.31-62

At last, the great day has arrived. Solomon's temple is complete, and Solomon stands before God and all the assembled people and prays.

His prayer shows how he hopes the temple will function: it is to be a place of certainty, where God's people know that they can pray and be heard. Solomon gives seven examples of the kind of need that will bring people to the temple – and they cover pretty well every contingency he could think of. When people fight, or sin against God, or go to war, or suffer drought or famine, they can come to the temple. So strong is God's commitment to those who pray in the temple, that even foreigners will be heard. The temple will even work long-distance for those who cannot physically reach it.

But, although Solomon loves the temple, he knows it is only a symbol. It does not bind God, but only reflects him. God has already shown himself to be a God who keeps his promise to Israel. The temple, like the covenant with Moses, shows God's love. God is already committed to his people.

Don't miss the warning note at the end of this passage: God's people must also be committed to God. Solomon, even in his rejoicing, knows that the temple is about a two-way relationship.

COLLECT

God, who in generous mercy sent the Holy Spirit
    upon your Church in the burning fire of your love:
grant that your people may be fervent
in the fellowship of the gospel
that, always abiding in you,
they may be found steadfast in faith and active in service;
through Jesus Christ your Son our Lord,
who is alive and reigns with you,
in the unity of the Holy Spirit,
one God, now and for ever.

Ordinary Time

Psalms 32, **36**
1 Kings 8.63 – 9.9
Acts 16.25-end

Tuesday 2 September

1 Kings 8.63 – 9.9

The dedication of Solomon's new temple is a high point of unity for the nation. After all the sacrifices, and after all the partying, the people go home, rejoicing. They know that God loves their king, and that that love guarantees their own stability as a nation and their own status before God. They go home completely happy. As far as they are concerned, that's all sewn up.

But Solomon cannot so easily believe that he has fulfilled all his responsibilities. In the aftermath of all the crowds and all the emotion and religious fervour, God comes to speak to Solomon again. The servants are still sweeping up the debris and sharing out the offerings when God comes to remind Solomon of just what the great temple is and what it is not.

God and Solomon are agreed that the temple is to be the centre of the relationship between God and Israel. The God who made the earth promises that his eyes and his heart will always be there, in the temple. And that means that God will see with terrible clarity exactly how his people are living and worshipping. If they do not respond to God with love and faithfulness, God's presence with them will be a terror, not a comfort.

COLLECT

Lord God,
defend your Church from all false teaching
and give to your people knowledge of your truth,
that we may enjoy eternal life
in Jesus Christ our Lord.

Ordinary Time

Wednesday 3 September

Psalm **34**
1 Kings 10.1-25
Acts 17.1-15

1 Kings 10.1-25

The people for whom this sequence of books from Joshua to 2 Kings was originally compiled would not remember the united Israel in its glory days. Whether the 'Deuteronomist' – the theologian or school of theologians responsible for the narrative's final shape – lived just before or just after the Exile of the people in the sixth century BC, the nation that they knew was divided and harassed by its more powerful neighbours.

So, to read about the days of Solomon is an exercise both in nostalgia and in hope. This is how God intended his people to be – and they can be so again, if only they will learn faithfulness. They can again be so powerful, rich and wise that exotic foreigners like the Queen of Sheba will be drawn by their fame.

This queen is the stuff of legends. She is there to evoke wealth and grandeur, with her spices and her jewels. She is there to magnify Solomon's status, since hers, although so great, is insignificant compared to his.

But she comes because Solomon has won the favour of Israel's God. The kingdom, the power and the glory come from God, and the Queen of Sheba knows it. Centuries after her death, this will win 'the Queen of the South' her commendation from Jesus (cf. Matthew 12.42).

COLLECT

God, who in generous mercy sent the Holy Spirit
   upon your Church in the burning fire of your love:
grant that your people may be fervent
in the fellowship of the gospel
that, always abiding in you,
they may be found steadfast in faith and active in service;
through Jesus Christ your Son our Lord,
who is alive and reigns with you,
in the unity of the Holy Spirit,
one God, now and for ever.

Ordinary Time

Psalm 37*
1 Kings 11.1-13
Acts 17.16-end

Thursday 4 September

1 Kings 11.1-13

In the previous chapter, Solomon is at his height. He excels all the kings of the earth, we are told, not just in wealth, but also in wisdom. But, while the story revels in the luxury of what it is describing, the insistent note of warning is never absent. All of this is God's gift, not Solomon's right.

But now Solomon's wisdom begins to desert him, and love begins to cloud his judgement, just as it did his father's. Solomon is born out of the illicit love of David for Bathsheba, but even that seems tame compared with boundaries that Solomon transgresses for love. For Solomon is indiscriminate in his loves, and his wives and concubines do not share his faith or his nationality.

Gradually, he comes to believe that, because he loves them, they can do no wrong. Gradually, he gets drawn into their religious practices, to the point where he himself, who built the temple where God lives, now builds altars to other gods.

All along, the consummate storyteller has made us see the fragility of Solomon's grandeur. It depended upon God, and now God will withdraw it. Solomon will not pay the price, but his child and his nation will.

COLLECT

Lord God,
defend your Church from all false teaching
and give to your people knowledge of your truth,
that we may enjoy eternal life
in Jesus Christ our Lord.

Ordinary Time

Friday 5 September

Psalm 31
1 Kings 11.26-end
Acts 18.1-21

1 Kings 11.26-end

This is when it becomes clear that the author or editor of 1 Kings is only peripherally interested in history. He is primarily a theologian, and his purpose in recounting past events is to see God's hand at work and try to draw out the lessons for himself and his readers.

So, Jeroboam's rebellion is so squeezed as to be almost incomprehensible, while the actions and words of Ahijah the prophet are told in great detail. Jeroboam comes to the attention of the king when overseeing the rebuilding of some of the city's defensive walls and putting up a 'millo', which was some kind of fortified structure. But we are told nothing of Jeroboam's supporters or his preparations for rebellion. Instead, we hear the prophet announcing, with the symbolic tearing of his garment, that Israel is to be divided, and that God's promises to David will not automatically follow David's line in every generation.

For the author, that is the end of Solomon. He has lost God's favour, and so his story is of no more interest. He refers the fact-obsessed to 'the Acts of Solomon' – a record we no longer possess. But he has told us all he thinks we need to know about this great king who forgot the source of his rule.

COLLECT

God, who in generous mercy sent the Holy Spirit
    upon your Church in the burning fire of your love:
grant that your people may be fervent
in the fellowship of the gospel
that, always abiding in you,
they may be found steadfast in faith and active in service;
through Jesus Christ your Son our Lord,
who is alive and reigns with you,
in the unity of the Holy Spirit,
one God, now and for ever.

Ordinary Time

Psalms 41, **42**, 43
1 Kings 12.1-24
Acts 18.22 – 19.7

Saturday 6 September

1 Kings 12.1-24

The nation over which David and Solomon had reigned was not a natural union. David had started off as king only of the southern part of it, Judah, and 2 Samuel tells us that it took him seven years to bring the northern part, Israel, into union. Solomon's great temple in Jerusalem, the southern part of the kingdom, was partly designed to strengthen the northern provinces' commitment to the united country.

After the death of Solomon, his son Rehoboam has to go north, to Shechem, to have his kingship accepted by the northerners of Israel. But they decide that if he is going to be their king, it has to be on their terms. No southern king is going to tell them what to do any longer.

The greybeards advise Rehoboam to accept the northerners' terms. They can see how volatile the situation is and that the future of the united kingdom is at stake. But Rehoboam has not inherited his father's famed wisdom. He grew up seeing the country as one, and expecting to rule it. He is not going to be told what to do by a bunch of peasants. So, David's hard-won kingdom is split apart by a boastful boy. Solomon's unfaithfulness is beginning to take effect, dividing God's people and their witness.

COLLECT

Lord God,
defend your Church from all false teaching
and give to your people knowledge of your truth,
that we may enjoy eternal life
in Jesus Christ our Lord.

Ordinary Time

Monday 8 September

Psalm **44**
1 Kings 12.25 – 13.10
Acts 19.8-20

1 Kings 12.25 – 13.10

Shechem was a significant place. It was in the northern part of the kingdom, and it was associated with some of the great religious heroes of the whole people of Israel and Judah. For example, Abraham was said to have built an altar to God at Shechem (see Genesis 12.6-8), and Joseph's bones were buried there (see Joshua 24.32).

So, Jeroboam is wise to make it the capital of his breakaway kingdom. He fully understood the significance of Jerusalem, and how easily people might go on thinking of it as their city and their temple. But Jeroboam makes the mistake of trying to set up not just a rival capital and worship centre, but also rival gods – local and tribal ones – associated with the old numinous places.

Jeroboam has already had one encounter with a prophet, in chapter 11. That one told Jeroboam that he was to benefit from God's anger with Solomon. Jeroboam should have learned that God's favour is vital to successful rule. Now the unnamed 'man of God' comes to warn Jeroboam that, even if the kingdom is split, there is still only one God.

The witness of the Bible and of history is that kings find it hard to remember that their power is not intrinsic to them.

COLLECT

O Lord, we beseech you mercifully to hear the prayers
    of your people who call upon you;
and grant that they may both perceive and know
    what things they ought to do,
and also may have grace and power faithfully to fulfil them;
through Jesus Christ your Son our Lord,
who is alive and reigns with you,
in the unity of the Holy Spirit,
one God, now and for ever.

Ordinary Time

Psalms **48**, 52
1 Kings 13.11-end
Acts 19.21-end

Tuesday 9 September

1 Kings 13.11-end

The old prophet had got out of the habit of believing that God really spoke through him. He had become accustomed to saying 'God says', when all he really meant was 'I think'. So he hears about the words and actions of the younger man, condemning Jeroboam's false religious practices, and sets out to meet another member of the guild. Prophets should stick together. He overrules the young man's scruples as ridiculous. God doesn't really go about telling people things.

He is taken aback at God's message at the dinner table, but doesn't allow it to disrupt the meal, and he waves off the younger man with no shadow on his conscience. But, when he hears of the young man's death and sees the strange sight of the lion and the donkey, faithfully standing guard, resisting their own natures, so as to do God's bidding, he realizes what he has done. And he realizes that the young man's prophecy about the consequences of Jeroboam's religious unfaithfulness will come true. Not much consolation for the young prophet, perhaps, to be vindicated after such a horrible death.

Perhaps the old prophet's previous indifference to his calling is partly to blame for the fact that Jeroboam is still unconvinced. But Jeroboam's taste for power could have something to do with it.

> Lord of creation,
> whose glory is around and within us:
> open our eyes to your wonders,
> that we may serve you with reverence
> and know your peace at our lives' end,
> through Jesus Christ our Lord.

COLLECT

Ordinary Time

Wednesday 10 September

Psalm **119.57-80**
1 Kings 17
Acts 20.1-16

1 Kings 17

We have skipped a few generations since yesterday's readings. There have been several kings of Israel since Jeroboam, and most of them have been condemned for doing evil in God's sight and making their people sin too. But Ahab, the one we are about to meet, is the worst of the lot. It may be his misfortune, or it may be God's providence, that one of Israel's worst kings is about to tangle with one of Israel's mightiest prophets, Elijah the Tishbite.

Elijah is sent to tell Ahab and his Baal-worshipping wife, Jezebel, that, because of their wickedness, there is going to be a terrible drought. But while the rest of the land suffers, God provides for his servant Elijah. And Elijah's faithfulness is to benefit others as well.

The widow who shares her last few morsels with Elijah does so out of despair rather than hope. If it is their last meal, it doesn't matter much, either way.

Although no doubt she is grateful for the miraculous multiplication of their food supply while Elijah is with them, it isn't until Elijah gives her back her son that she really believes he is God's prophet. Anyone can feed you, but only God can give you your heart's desire.

COLLECT

O Lord, we beseech you mercifully to hear the prayers
    of your people who call upon you;
and grant that they may both perceive and know
    what things they ought to do,
and also may have grace and power faithfully to fulfil them;
through Jesus Christ your Son our Lord,
who is alive and reigns with you,
in the unity of the Holy Spirit,
one God, now and for ever.

Ordinary Time

Psalms 56, **57** (63*)
1 Kings 18.1-20
Acts 20.17-end

Thursday 11 September

1 Kings 18.1-20

This is masterly storytelling. In a very few words, the author tells us what has been happening since we last met Elijah. The drought has been going on for three years, and even the king is not able to protect himself and his prized horses from its effects. Jezebel has been pursuing a vendetta – presumably with her husband's connivance – against God's prophets. And everyone has been scouring the land and the surrounding countries for Elijah. Because he prophesied the drought, he is blamed for it.

But the narrative heart of the passage is in the dialogue, first between Elijah and Obadiah, and then between Elijah and Ahab. Obadiah's testimony suggests that Ahab is deeply divided. He allows Jezebel to persecute the prophets, but he still employs a man who has defied Jezebel. Obadiah's loyalties are divided, too. But he is in no doubt about Elijah's power or Ahab's temper, and who will bear the brunt of both. Elijah will vanish again, and Ahab will take it out on him. Crossing the queen is just about all right, but annoying the king is another matter.

So, at last, after three years, king and prophet confront each other. Ahab has persuaded himself that everything is Elijah's fault, but, in a few swift words, Elijah disabuses him of that notion and stands ready to prove it.

COLLECT

Lord of creation,
whose glory is around and within us:
open our eyes to your wonders,
that we may serve you with reverence
and know your peace at our lives' end,
through Jesus Christ our Lord.

Ordinary Time

Friday 12 September

Psalms **51**, 54
1 Kings 18.21-end
Acts 21.1-16

1 Kings 18.21-end

Elijah goes right to the heart of the matter, and his words are not only for the people but also for Ahab. Who is God? The people have been hedging their bets, making offerings both to Baal and to Israel's Lord. So Elijah is here to prove that that is nonsense. If God really is God, then there is no need to try to placate other powers. Worship and offerings to other 'gods' are a complete waste of time.

The scene is described so brilliantly that there is really no need for any commentator to gild the lily. First, there are the prophets of Baal, all energy, noise and spectacle, trying to ignore the grim, mocking figure of Elijah, just standing there watching them. Right to the last moment, they go on hoping that their frantic efforts will at least keep the people's loyalty and attention, even if not Baal's.

But one word from Elijah, and everyone turns to watch him instead. There is no obvious excitement here, as Elijah slowly and deliberately makes his preparations. But, unlike the prophets of Baal, Elijah does not believe he is the main attraction. God is the one who does the spectacular, not Elijah.

So, now is it clear who is God?

COLLECT

O Lord, we beseech you mercifully to hear the prayers
    of your people who call upon you;
and grant that they may both perceive and know
    what things they ought to do,
and also may have grace and power faithfully to fulfil them;
through Jesus Christ your Son our Lord,
who is alive and reigns with you,
in the unity of the Holy Spirit,
one God, now and for ever.

Ordinary Time

Psalm **68**
1 Kings 19
Acts 21.17-36

Saturday 13 September

1 Kings 19

For Jezebel, religion is a matter of authority – her own. She does not care whether or not people believe in Baal. The point is, they must act as she tells them. So it is no excuse to say that Elijah's God has just proved himself beyond any doubt. Until Jezebel tells them differently, Baal is god.

Elijah has never had any illusions about his own importance. When he is doing God's work, he is invulnerable and wholly authoritative. But the rest of the time, he's a human being. So he runs from Jezebel's fury. Yet again, having delivered God's message, Elijah is homeless and friendless, and now he is very tired.

But even in his weariness and longing for release, he knows his God. Unnecessary noise and display is not God's way, so it is only when the deep silence arrives that Elijah comes out to talk to God.

So many times we have heard Elijah deliver God's message to others. Now we hear God speaking directly and personally to his faithful servant, addressing him by name. The God who struck as a holocaust on Mount Carmel listens patiently to Elijah's complaints, and promises him release. Just a few more tasks, and then Elijah will get the rest he longs for.

> Lord of creation,
> whose glory is around and within us:
> open our eyes to your wonders,
> that we may serve you with reverence
> and know your peace at our lives' end,
> through Jesus Christ our Lord.

COLLECT

Ordinary Time

Monday 15 September

Psalm **71**
1 Kings 21
Acts 21.37 – 22.21

1 Kings 21

King Ahab and Queen Jezebel are interesting character studies. Like Macbeth and his wife, each knows the other's strengths and weaknesses. But, although Jezebel's name resounds through history as a synonym for vice, it is Ahab, the much more nuanced and divided character, who actually drives the relationship. Ahab knows exactly what to do to get the reaction he wants out of Jezebel.

So, when he goes to complain to her about Naboth, he leaves out several important details in the conversation he has just had. Naboth invokes both God and the law in refusing to part with his vineyard. Both God and the law of inheritance have made the land his. But Ahab only tells Jezebel about the refusal to sell for money, making it sound a petty and unreasonable denial of the king. Then he sits back and waits for her to get him what he wants.

Ahab does recognize Elijah as God's true spokesman. He treats him with a mixture of respect and hatred that shows the fault line in his character. He does know God, but he wishes that God was more like Jezebel and would simply give him everything he wants. Ahab and Jezebel believe that kingship is about power, but, unfortunately for them, God does not agree.

COLLECT

Almighty God,
you have made us for yourself,
and our hearts are restless till they find their rest in you:
pour your love into our hearts and draw us to yourself,
and so bring us at last to your heavenly city
where we shall see you face to face;
through Jesus Christ your Son our Lord,
who is alive and reigns with you,
in the unity of the Holy Spirit,
one God, now and for ever.

Ordinary Time

Psalm **73**
1 Kings 22.1-28

Tuesday 16 September

1 Kings 22.1-28

One of the themes running through 1 Kings is prophecy. Clearly, there were 'professional' prophets in Israel at the time, some attached to the cult of Baal, and some calling themselves the Lord's prophets. But it sounds as though many of them saw this primarily as a court position, whose main duty was to agree with the king, and whose chief qualification was an ability to work out what it was that the king wanted to hear.

The trouble for these 'yes-prophets' was that there were also true prophets, who really did only say what the Lord had given them to say, and that the king knew the difference. So in today's story, the well-meaning prophets are put in an impossible position. They have to say what the king wants to hear, but they know that they will not be believed.

Not that Micaiah is in a much better position. The king says he wants the truth, but he also wants the truth to be good news. So if Micaiah only says what God has given him to say, he is going to be in trouble both with his fellow-prophets and with the king.

But true prophets and false prophets alike will be judged by history, though, obviously, it is only Micaiah who troubles to point this out.

COLLECT

Gracious God,
you call us to fullness of life:
deliver us from unbelief
and banish our anxieties
with the liberating love of Jesus Christ our Lord.

Ordinary Time

Wednesday 17 September

Psalm **77**
1 Kings 22.29-45
Acts 23.12-end

1 Kings 22.29-45

It is hard to tell if the king of Israel was a coward or a hero. He could have been going into battle in disguise to mingle with the ordinary soldiers and take his chances of life and death with them, without the added protection afforded to a king. Or he could have known that he was the prime target and hoped that the enemy did not know the difference between him and the king of Judah. When he was wounded, he could have instructed his men to strap him to his chariot so that his side were not disheartened by the sight of his death, or he could have been unable to get out of the press of battle and simply bled to death by accident. It is the first half of the chapter that makes the less heroic option the probable one. Micaiah has warned the king of Israel that he will not win, and the king knows, however reluctantly, that Micaiah is a true prophet.

Quite suddenly, we learn that this king of Israel is Ahab, meeting the doom that Elijah predicted. But the division between 1 Kings and 2 Kings is arbitrary. Read on to see Jezebel get her reward, and find out what happens next to Israel and Judah's kings.

COLLECT

Almighty God,
you have made us for yourself,
and our hearts are restless till they find their rest in you:
pour your love into our hearts and draw us to yourself,
and so bring us at last to your heavenly city
where we shall see you face to face;
through Jesus Christ your Son our Lord,
who is alive and reigns with you,
in the unity of the Holy Spirit,
one God, now and for ever.

Ordinary Time

Psalm **78.1-39***
2 Kings 1.2-17
Acts 24.1-23

Thursday 18 September

2 Kings 1.2-17

Stories like this are best understood as legends. That does not mean that they do not have a basis in real history. The formidable Elijah, with his relentless and costly campaign for the exclusive claims of Yahweh, is certainly no legendary invention.

Here, his story is told in a legendary stylized form that underlines its main point by over-simplification and exaggeration, so that what it wants to say may be unmistakably clear – as a cartoon might do nowadays.

Its powerful warning is that there is a true religion that relates you to a living God, and there is a false religion that relates you to an unreal God – and those, like the king and his hapless captains, who are on the wrong side have no future. In stark contrast, Elijah, although in a seemingly helpless minority, serves a living God who will authenticate what he does in his name.

Amid all the hard questions that such a story raises, we would do well to let it remind us that, for all our contemporary preoccupation with religious pluralism, faith can be either death-dealing or life-giving, and to heed its call to be careful about where we take our stand.

> Gracious God,
> you call us to fullness of life:
> deliver us from unbelief
> and banish our anxieties
> with the liberating love of Jesus Christ our Lord.

COLLECT

Ordinary Time

Friday 19 September

Psalm **55**
2 Kings 2.1-18
Acts 24.24 – 25.12

2 Kings 2.1-18

Handing over to a successor is often an uneasy business – and that uneasiness hangs over this passage when Elijah is going to have to hand over to Elisha his work and his place in God's plan.

Elisha is far more keen on keeping close to Elijah than Elijah is to encouraging the young man's determined companionship. He wants to make his own, while he still can, all that Elijah has to give him; he hopes that, by staying close to the master, he will perhaps inherit the mantle and the power that will part the Jordan and prove that the Lord is with him. 'Let me inherit a double share of your spirit.'

Elijah is reluctant; he tries to be rid of Elisha, perhaps because he is preoccupied with his own coming demise, perhaps because he cannot bear the thought of handing over to another what has filled his own life for so long.

But, when the decisive moment comes, Elijah at last surrenders his ministry to Elisha and finds that what awaits him is not dreaded death, but a new future with the God who is as faithful to him as he has been to God.

Predecessors and successors, take note!

COLLECT

Almighty God,
you have made us for yourself,
and our hearts are restless till they find their rest in you:
pour your love into our hearts and draw us to yourself,
and so bring us at last to your heavenly city
where we shall see you face to face;
through Jesus Christ your Son our Lord,
who is alive and reigns with you,
in the unity of the Holy Spirit,
one God, now and for ever.

Ordinary Time

Psalms **76**, 79
2 Kings 4.1-37
Acts 25.13-end

Saturday 20 September

2 Kings 4.1-37

Once more, legendary stories make pertinent points. Elijah and Elisha are both political prophets concerned with great national issues, most of all Israel's covenant faithfulness to God.

But the political remains distant apart from the personal. Social campaigns without pastoral concerns can mean caring for everybody in general but nobody in particular.

However, Elisha, like Elijah earlier, knows how to be pastoral; here, he is at his most personal and, indeed, most attractive in the way he responds to two women confronted with three of the fundamental concerns of life: the need for food, the need for children and the threat of death.

In making the widow's jar of oil outlast the famine, and the Shunammite woman fertile, he simply deploys the remarkable powers that God has given him at no cost to himself.

But, when the child's death has to be challenged, he has to go in person to convey to the child's body breath from his own body. By his intimate, self-giving embrace of what is dead, life is restored. For Elisha – as later for Jesus – it is as he comes and gives himself to us, one by one, in our deadness that we come to new life in him.

> Gracious God,
> you call us to fullness of life:
> deliver us from unbelief
> and banish our anxieties
> with the liberating love of Jesus Christ our Lord.

COLLECT

Ordinary Time

Monday 22 September

Psalms **80**, 82
2 Kings 5
Acts 26.1-23

2 Kings 5

Getting into God's healing zone often means getting out of our own comfort zone, as this story shows. A slave girl has to lift her head from cleaning floors to refer her sick master to the right consultant. A king has to turn from politics to ask one of his vassals to facilitate the healing of his leading general.

It is hardest of all for Naaman and Elisha. Elisha has to learn how to be inclusive and generous to a threatening stranger without compromising his own faith and calling. He will indeed heal Naaman, but he has to seek that healing by a baptism in Israel's river and at the hand of Israel's God.

For Naaman himself, it is hardest of all. He has to go into an alien culture and submit himself to the ministry of a man whom he would have considered his natural enemy. He certainly does not like the prescription that is offered to him, with its claim that the rivers and the God of Israel have a saving power far beyond those of Syria. But the reward of such humiliation is more than healing – it is conversion to the living God.

COLLECT

Almighty and everlasting God,
increase in us your gift of faith
that, forsaking what lies behind
and reaching out to that which is before,
we may run the way of your commandments
and win the crown of everlasting joy;
through Jesus Christ your Son our Lord,
who is alive and reigns with you,
in the unity of the Holy Spirit,
one God, now and for ever.

Ordinary Time

Psalms 87, **89.1-18**
2 Kings 6.1-23
Acts 26.24-end

Tuesday 23 September

2 Kings 6.1-23

Relationships are constantly being reshaped by circumstances. We have seen Elisha in positive mode towards a Syrian general on the personal level – but now, on the political level, he is conducting a campaign of supernatural espionage against Syria's king. That king, in turn, who had been looking to Elisha for healing, now in anger sends a large army against him to finish him off.

But the same God who had healed Naaman now defeats the Syrian army with an even stronger force of his own, so that blinded soldiers are led off to captivity and probable death.

Once again, the story takes a strange turn. Elisha, who has been the undoing of the army, becomes personally compassionate to the soldiers that comprise it by insisting that, instead of being slaughtered, they should be fed and sent home.

Great causes often mean that we have to oppose and resist the people who try to hinder and frustrate them, but political opposition must not be allowed to turn into personal animosity; we do not surrender to those who seek our undoing, but we still cherish them personally and do them good whenever we can. Loving your enemies – that is the name of the game!

COLLECT

God, our judge and saviour,
teach us to be open to your truth
and to trust in your love,
that we may live each day
with confidence in the salvation which is given
through Jesus Christ our Lord.

Ordinary Time

Wednesday 24 September

Psalm **119.105-128**
2 Kings 9.1-16
Acts 27.1-26

2 Kings 9.1-16

Tyrannical regimes do not last for ever in a world where the God of Israel is in control, and his just judgements have the last word over the violent injustice of seemingly powerful rulers. Here, God is at work undermining the royal house of Ahab, which has deserted him for more accommodating gods who will legitimate its injustices.

The regime is attacked both from within and from without. Tyrannies carry in themselves the seeds of their own destruction. Ahab's son, Joram, is sinking under the weight of his father's wrongdoing, and neither his kingly status nor his attempted alliances, nor his armed might, can now save his skin.

But, if Joram is the weary king who has run out of steam, Jehu is the young champion whom God has raised up for his undoing. The next passage tells us that he drove his chariot in a way that broke all the speed limits (v.20) – and that is a sign of the vigour, energy and resilience that he brings to his task.

When the man who comes from the corrupt past is collapsing, God brings in the new man who will clear the ground for a new future ahead.

COLLECT

Almighty and everlasting God,
increase in us your gift of faith
that, forsaking what lies behind
and reaching out to that which is before,
we may run the way of your commandments
and win the crown of everlasting joy;
through Jesus Christ your Son our Lord,
who is alive and reigns with you,
in the unity of the Holy Spirit,
one God, now and for ever.

Ordinary Time

Psalm 90, **92**
2 Kings 9.17-end
Acts 27.27-end

Thursday 25 September

2 Kings 9.17-end

God has his pay days! You may deceive, murder and steal, as Ahab prompted by Jezebel did in Naboth's vineyard, but, by the explicit decree of a righteous divine providence, the son is the victim of a violent death in the very same place that the father committed a violent murder.

Nor is there any escape for Queen Jezebel, who did not commit the original crime but most certainly inspired it. She puts on her make-up for the last time (v.30), but her battlements cannot protect her from the just retribution that seeks her out and brings her to a horrible end.

This story is so offensive to all our modern susceptibilities that we find it hard to hear what it is saying to us. We want a God of love to bring everything to a happy ending. But, when people like the Ahab family live lives and pursue policies that utterly reject that love, the point will come when that love, to be true to itself, will have to reject their lovelessness and hand them over to the destructive violence by which they have lived and must now die.

COLLECT

God, our judge and saviour,
teach us to be open to your truth
and to trust in your love,
that we may live each day
with confidence in the salvation which is given
through Jesus Christ our Lord.

Ordinary Time

Friday 26 September

Psalms **88**, (95)
2 Kings 12.1-19
Acts 28.1-16

2 Kings 12.1-19

Altars need temples, and temples need repairs. The priests who may be first-rate about the rituals are not necessarily competent or even trustworthy about the repairs. This passage is about church finance – something that can vex us all. Here, the problem is less about how to raise the money but more about how to spend it.

The practically minded king has a hard time of it with recalcitrant clergy who are spending the offerings on their own unidentified pet projects and are very reluctant to organize a much-needed programme of building repairs. The king must therefore organize a special collection for a fabric fund that will be handed over to competent lay people who will make sure that the services can continue without the roof leaking.

To be the treasurer or a member of the finance committee may not look very spiritual, but the spiritual things may not prosper very long if the finances are in a mess or in the wrong, even if ordained, hands. In his list of charismatic gifts in 1 Corinthians 12, Paul lists helping and administrating – and the Lord has much need of them. King Jehoash would have agreed!

COLLECT

Almighty and everlasting God,
increase in us your gift of faith
that, forsaking what lies behind
and reaching out to that which is before,
we may run the way of your commandments
and win the crown of everlasting joy;
through Jesus Christ your Son our Lord,
who is alive and reigns with you,
in the unity of the Holy Spirit,
one God, now and for ever.

Ordinary Time

Psalms 96, **97**, 100
2 Kings 17.1-23
Acts 28.17-end

Saturday 27 September

2 Kings 17.1-23

We move down the years to the final dénouement for the kingdom of Israel. Now the judgement of rejection that previously assailed a single royal family falls on the whole nation as it goes into exile and disappears from history.

This is the people whom God, in his love, liberated from Egypt to be the bearers of his name and his purpose. But, since David and Solomon, there has been a long decline into national apostasy, which neither reforming kings nor God's patient willingness to give them yet another chance were able to reverse.

Now their time is up. The worship of Yahweh is still the established religion, but the heart of the people is no longer in it. Their love and their devotion have gone to other more congenial gods, and the ways of the Lord are followed no more. Generations of prophets have warned them repeatedly of a coming judgement but have gone unheeded. Now the end has come, and the people who entered the Promised Land in joy and freedom are marched off to Assyria in the chains of slavery.

Those who persist in rejecting God are at risk of becoming a rejected people.

> God, our judge and saviour,
> teach us to be open to your truth
> and to trust in your love,
> that we may live each day
> with confidence in the salvation which is given
> through Jesus Christ our Lord.

COLLECT

Ordinary Time

Monday 29 September

Michael and All Angels

Psalms 34, 150
Daniel 12.1-4
Acts 12.1-11

Daniel 12.1-4

Angels are the neon lights on God's messages and God's purposes. When he has something to which he specially wants to draw our attention, they appear to highlight it, as they did in the fields at Bethlehem and the empty tomb of Easter.

Their function is never to speak of or for themselves, but to be the faithful heralds of the message that God has entrusted to them – and we honour them best when we pay heed to the gospel they are sent to convey.

In their heavenly calling, we can see the prototype of our earthly mission. Our function also is so to live and speak that we floodlight the gospel in a way that enables others to heed and receive it.

This passage points to another, even more mysterious, angelic ministry. The Archangel Michael is appointed the heavenly patron and protector of Israel, and Jesus hints that God has allocated such an angelic guardian to each of us (Matthew 18.10). Just as we are helped and protected in ways we can see by good friends on earth, so our interests will be looked after in ways beyond our knowing in the hidden realms of heaven.

COLLECT

Everlasting God,
you have ordained and constituted
    the ministries of angels and mortals in a wonderful order:
grant that as your holy angels always serve you in heaven,
so, at your command,
they may help and defend us on earth;
through Jesus Christ your Son our Lord,
who is alive and reigns with you,
in the unity of the Holy Spirit,
one God, now and for ever.

Ordinary Time

Psalms **106*** (or 103)
2 Kings 18.1-12
Philippians 1.12-end

Tuesday 30 September

Philippians 1.12-end

Where we are most loved, we can be most open. That is perhaps why this letter to the church with which he had the most affectionate and untroubled relationship is the one in which Paul can pull aside the veil of personal reticence.

In this passage, he gives us glimpses into his realistic but hopeful reaction to his Roman imprisonment and its possible outcome. His chief concern is not for his own comfort and release, but for the way in which his time in prison is serving the interests of the gospel.

In prison, he has made an unlikely contact with the upper echelons of the imperial military establishment (v.13); his enforced silence has energized others to speak for Christ, even if their motives for so doing are mixed and imperfect.

He faces squarely two possible outcomes, release or execution, and finds reason for hope in both (v.20). If he dies, he will be with Christ – the best personal outcome – but release will mean the continuation of his mission, and, because that will be best for his churches, he is sure that it will happen.

Personal troubles thus exposed to the light of Christ will yield good reasons for hope.

> Faithful Lord,
> whose steadfast love never ceases
> and whose mercies never come to an end:
> grant us the grace to trust you
> and to receive the gifts of your love,
> new every morning,
> in Jesus Christ our Lord.

COLLECT

Ordinary Time

Wednesday 1 October

Psalms 110, 111, 112
2 Kings 18.13-end
Philippians 2.1-13

Philippians 2.1-13

A full response to Jesus Christ involves the worship of our hearts, the enagagement of our minds and the obedience of our lives. In this glorious passage, all three cohere.

Most scholars think that here Paul is either quoting or adapting a hymn that would be familiar to his readers as part of the worship of the earliest Church (vv.6-11). This is a theology that cannot but set us singing. It acclaims one who shared God's being but in love humbled himself to share ours, and who, for our sakes, shouldered the whole burden and consequence of our suffering and sin. As a result, he has been exalted to share God's name and God's worship so that the whole human future is in his hands.

To worship such a Christ must mean that the shape of his life should become the shape of ours. We are not to be like the first Adam who grabbed at an equality with God he could never attain, but like this second Adam who possessed this equality but used it not to exalt himself but to love us.

'Let the same mind be in you' (v.5).

COLLECT

O God, forasmuch as without you
we are not able to please you;
mercifully grant that your Holy Spirit
may in all things direct and rule our hearts;
through Jesus Christ your Son our Lord,
who is alive and reigns with you,
in the unity of the Holy Spirit,
one God, now and for ever.

Ordinary Time

Psalms 113, **115**
2 Kings 19.1-19
Philippians 2.14-end

Thursday 2 October

Philippians 2.14-end

It is one thing to write a letter, but quite another to send a friend. Paul and the Philippians kept in touch by exchanging not just written words but personal representatives.

They sent him Epaphroditus with a gift to meet Paul's needs, and Paul, in turn, has been looking after him in his illness (v.27). Now he is sending him back with the promise that he will soon be followed by Timothy, who is as close to Paul as a good son to a good father, and will be able to help them as well as he would himself.

Of course, it would be even better if he could come himself (v.24), but until then, he can be present and active not just in person but through a representative who knows his mind and carries his authority.

To send a letter rather than make a visit can be all too easy, but the fellowship of the gospel is maintained by personal exchanges, not just by written words. God's final word to us was spoken by the coming of his Son, who bore his authority and brought his salvation. So, don't just write a letter, go yourself or send a friend.

COLLECT

Faithful Lord,
whose steadfast love never ceases
and whose mercies never come to an end:
grant us the grace to trust you
and to receive the gifts of your love,
new every morning,
in Jesus Christ our Lord.

Ordinary Time

Friday 3 October

Psalm **139**
2 Kings 19.20-36
Philippians 3.1 – 4.1

Philippians 3.1 – 4.1

This passage records Paul's conversion from complacent self-satisfaction to unsatisfied but confident ambition.

Paul has often been presented as a man who was increasingly dissatisfied with his Jewish faith until he found full satisfaction in Christ – but that is not the story he tells here. On the contrary, before his conversion, he was completely content with his first-class Jewish credentials and moral attainments (v.6). Now, however, his meeting with Christ has totally overturned his religious applecart. The old sources of his security, exposed to the judgement of Jesus, are now seen to be 'rubbish', as the NRSV puts it. Now his standing with God depends not on his Jewish background and moral conformity, but on his faith in what Jesus has done for him.

That confident faith, far from founding a new complacency, has inspired a new and restless ambition. Having discovered the unsuspected riches that there are in Christ, his chief aim in life is to press urgently and hopefully along Christ's way of cross and resurrection until he comes to full possession of them.

A defining characteristic of an authentic faith in the genuine Jesus is that what we have from him already makes us hungry and ambitious for more.

COLLECT

O God, forasmuch as without you
we are not able to please you;
mercifully grant that your Holy Spirit
may in all things direct and rule our hearts;
through Jesus Christ your Son our Lord,
who is alive and reigns with you,
in the unity of the Holy Spirit,
one God, now and for ever.

Ordinary Time

Psalms 120, **121**, 122
2 Kings 20
Philippians 4.2-end

Saturday 4 October

Philippians 4.2-end

Into the middle of this passage (vv.4-7), Paul inserts, if not a full recipe for worship, some clear and important clues for prayer.

He tells us first that, when we are praying, we should always start with God. Before we turn to the burden of the needs that we bring, we should joyfully acknowledge the already experienced grace and generosity of the God to whom we bring them. So not once, but twice, he bids us to 'rejoice in the Lord'.

In the presence of that God, we can then dare to ask for what we need. We are not to be too pious too soon and say to God what we think he would like to hear; we are to entrust him with the real desires of our hearts for others and ourselves and so let our requests be made known to God.

To such prayer there is promised 'the peace of God, which surpasses all understanding'. God will respond to that prayer in a way that leads us forward into that peace, that *shalom* of ultimate well-being, which is his will for us, even if often that leading is beyond our comprehension and outside our control.

COLLECT

Faithful Lord,
whose steadfast love never ceases
and whose mercies never come to an end:
grant us the grace to trust you
and to receive the gifts of your love,
new every morning,
in Jesus Christ our Lord.

Ordinary Time

Monday 6 October

Psalms 123, 124, 125, **126**
2 Kings 21.1-18
1 Timothy 1.1-17

1 Timothy 1.1-17

The local church has just started running a 'Christian Basics' course for people who want to find out more about what Christianity is all about. It would be strange if, at the first week's meeting, the leaders launched into a complicated explanation of some of the niceties of Anglican Canon Law. What they did start with were some church members giving short testimonies about what being a Christian has meant to them. They spoke of how following Jesus had brought love, joy and freedom into their daily living.

Paul knows that Timothy had to contend with 'certain people' in his church who focused on complicated theories and the strictness of the law. He calls this 'meaningless talk', contrasting it with the truth of the gospel. For Paul, the 'good news' is that he, previously a 'man of violence', has been rescued, redeemed and commissioned for ministry in Christ's service. The Christian basics are not, for Paul, about rules and regulations (amazing, given his strict religious background), conjecture or controversy, but are rather to do with 'a pure heart, a good conscience and sincere faith'. The source of all Christian teaching, and its aim, is the faith, love, mercy and patience that overflow from the heart of God. The challenge to each of us is to allow that every aspect of our life and ministry springs from these qualities too.

COLLECT

God, the giver of life,
whose Holy Spirit wells up within your Church:
by the Spirit's gifts equip us to live the gospel of Christ
    and make us eager to do your will,
that we may share with the whole creation
    the joys of eternal life;
through Jesus Christ your Son our Lord,
who is alive and reigns with you,
in the unity of the Holy Spirit,
one God, now and for ever.

Ordinary Time

Psalms **132**, 133
2 Kings 22.1 – 23.3
1 Timothy 1.18 – 2.end

Tuesday 7 October

1 Timothy 1.18 – 2.end

I have often wished that Paul had not included this bit in his letter. As an ordained woman who believes that my primary calling is to teach the faith, I have wrestled with these verses, alone and with others. But here it is. Can I even learn to live by its values?

At the time this letter was written, the goddess Diana (or Artemis) was worshipped by an all-female cult that excluded and denigrated men. Paul asks Christian men and women to model something different. He urges them not to conform to the stereotypes – that men are prone to 'anger or argument', and women are concerned only with 'gold, pearls or expensive clothes'. He suggests instead that men can be prayerful, and women can study and learn. And all of this is in the context of there being 'one God' and 'one mediator ... Christ Jesus'.

The weight behind this text, its 'value to live by', is that God does not condone the battle of the sexes. If Paul were writing his letter today, would he perhaps rail against the views that 'real men don't go to church' and 'real women can't be church leaders'? He might again warn men and women not to fall into limiting stereotypes, but instead to work together in godly partnership to build up the Church and live out the gospel.

COLLECT

God, our light and our salvation:
illuminate our lives,
that we may see your goodness in the land of the living,
and looking on your beauty
may be changed into the likeness of Jesus Christ our Lord.

Ordinary Time

Wednesday 8 October

Psalm **119.153-end**
2 Kings 23.4-25
1 Timothy 3

1 Timothy 3

A prominent theme of the letter to Timothy is the need for the church at Ephesus to be clearly distinguishable from ungodly cultures around it. Much of what is written is aimed at refuting 'certain people' (1.3), possibly gnostics, who had been spreading false doctrine. Here, Paul advocates a kind of leadership that is in contrast to these false teachers and 'stands out' as distinctive from the prevailing culture. Most of the qualities he espouses for bishops, deacons and female officers in the church are not exclusively Christian ones, but are to do with honour, reputation and good standing in the wider community.

To be a leader is to put oneself in a vulnerable position, a fact of which Paul is himself well aware. So, he aims to guide leaders into a way of living that has integrity and is secure and enriching, both for themselves and for the people for whom they have responsibility.

There is much discussion today about what it means to 'be church' – about 'fresh expressions of church' and 'new ways of doing church'. In this section of his letter to the young church at Ephesus, Paul puts these discussions into a wider context. He calls the church 'the household of God', 'the church of the living God' and 'the pillar and bulwark of the truth'. These are lofty descriptions and high callings. No wonder they require of their leaders the very highest standards.

COLLECT

God, the giver of life,
whose Holy Spirit wells up within your Church:
by the Spirit's gifts equip us to live the gospel of Christ
    and make us eager to do your will,
that we may share with the whole creation
    the joys of eternal life;
through Jesus Christ your Son our Lord,
who is alive and reigns with you,
in the unity of the Holy Spirit,
one God, now and for ever.

Ordinary Time

Psalms **143**, 146
2 Kings 23.36 – 24.17
1 Timothy 4

Thursday 9 October

1 Timothy 4

When I go to my local gym, I see people inflicting upon themselves great 'toil and struggle' on all manner of machines and contraptions that look as if they were designed as instruments of torture. And yet people keep on going back, keep on putting themselves through their paces. Why do they do it? Because eventually they see results. They look better. They feel healthier. They know it does them good. But it's hard work.

Some people have questioned Paul's authorship of the letter to Timothy, but 'toil and struggle' (v.10) is such a 'Pauline' expression. That phrase (or variations of it) appears six times in his epistles. This is because, for Paul, the Christian life is anything but a walk in the park. Real discipleship demands consistent effort in order to experience growth and results.

Physical fitness training is good for you, says Paul. But even better is spiritual fitness training; training in godliness. The apparatus that will help me train like this is not a treadmill or rowing machine, but the hard endeavour to live 'in love, in faith, in purity'. These things take time, practice and devotion before I will see progress – the spiritual equivalent of sweating it out, week in, week out. Add to all this a healthy diet of 'sound teaching' and 'words of the faith', and you have the spiritual fitness plan that will sustain and strengthen the Christian athlete.

COLLECT

God, our light and our salvation:
illuminate our lives,
that we may see your goodness in the land of the living,
and looking on your beauty
may be changed into the likeness of Jesus Christ our Lord.

Ordinary Time

Friday 10 October

Psalms 142, **144**
2 Kings 24.18 – 25.12
1 Timothy 5.1-16

1 Timothy 5.1-16

Yesterday, Paul urged Timothy not to let anyone 'despise his youth'. Today, we find the other side of that exhortation; Timothy is reminded to treat those who are of another generation with care and respect. In that society, older people would have relied on their immediate families for their support and care – there were no pension provisions. So, Paul issues strict directives about the obligations of family members to care for those in genuine need, especially widows. On top of that, in this new, radical Christian community, all people are to be viewed as family members – as sisters, brothers, mothers and fathers – and treated as such.

Last night's television news had two main headlines. One was about the problem of youth gangs on the streets of Britain. The other was about the neglect of elderly people in care homes. Perhaps Paul was on to something important in urging a greater degree of consideration and hospitality between the generations. J. B. Priestley is purported to have said: 'There was no respect for youth when I was young, and now that I am old, there is no respect for age – I missed it coming and going.' Paul suggests a different way of living and respecting, as necessary for good relating today as when it was first written.

COLLECT

God, the giver of life,
whose Holy Spirit wells up within your Church:
by the Spirit's gifts equip us to live the gospel of Christ
    and make us eager to do your will,
that we may share with the whole creation
    the joys of eternal life;
through Jesus Christ your Son our Lord,
who is alive and reigns with you,
in the unity of the Holy Spirit,
one God, now and for ever.

Ordinary Time

Psalm 147
2 Kings 25.22-end
1 Timothy 5.17-end

Saturday 11 October

1 Timothy 5.17-end

Theological colleges today have to attend to training outcomes and ministerial competencies for those training for ordained ministry, issued by the central authorities of the Church of England. These verses of Paul's letter can be seen as a similar set of guidelines. They contain practical advice to Timothy to help him lead and manage the elders of the church in their ministerial task. You get the impression that things had not always been straightforward in the team in the recent past and that the 'sins of some people' (v.24) are not hypothetical ones.

The guidance given by Paul is sensible and down to earth. He reiterates some basics about good teamworking – let people who do a good job be rewarded, don't falsely accuse each other, behave with integrity, don't have favourites. It's all common sense really, but it goes to show that teamwork in churches was as challenging and demanding then as it often is now.

For those of us who work in teams, whether in the Church or the secular workplace, and especially for those who lead them, the challenge is to be as straightforward and open as Paul encourages Timothy to be. In a culture where prejudice and partiality can all too easily be the hallmarks of the workplace, our task is to model honest, transparent relationships that are conspicuous in their goodness.

God, our light and our salvation:
illuminate our lives,
that we may see your goodness in the land of the living,
and looking on your beauty
may be changed into the likeness of Jesus Christ our Lord.

COLLECT

Ordinary Time

Monday 13 October

Psalms 1, 2, 3
Exodus 22.21-27
1 Timothy 6.1-10

1 Timothy 6.1-10

Our headlines, quiz shows and our media are increasingly money-focused – winning it, having it, making it, giving it, analyzing it, exploring it.

Hear the words of Paul: 'envy, dissension, slander, base suspicions, and wrangling among those who are depraved in mind and bereft of the truth …' Who is he describing? Dreadful axe-murderers? Sinful fornicators? Evil philanderers? None of these. Paul doesn't mince his words about people in the Church who are only in it for what they can get out, namely the money. These alarming attributes are contrasted with one simple trait: 'contentment'. Alfred Nobel described contentment as 'the only real wealth'. The content person is able to live contentedly in the moment and to focus on things that are more valuable than money ever will be; that person is rich indeed.

Paul professes elsewhere to have 'learned' contentment (Philippians 4.11-12), suggesting that contentment is not something that comes naturally. It has to be practised and worked on. More of Jesus' own teachings are about money and possessions than any other single topic. Surprising, maybe, but demonstrating that he too knew how easy it is for 'eagerness to be rich' to get in the way of contentedly following him.

COLLECT

Grant, we beseech you, merciful Lord,
to your faithful people pardon and peace,
that they may be cleansed from all their sins
and serve you with a quiet mind;
through Jesus Christ your Son our Lord,
who is alive and reigns with you,
in the unity of the Holy Spirit,
one God, now and for ever.

Ordinary Time

Psalms **5**, 6, (8)
Exodus 29.38 – 30.16
1 Timothy 6.11-end

Tuesday 14 October

1 Timothy 6.11-end

'Carpe diem', wrote the Latin poet, Horace. It's a phrase that has been widely used in popular culture and was a prominent theme in the film *Dead Poets Society*, in which teacher John Keating (played by Robin Williams) urges his pupils: *'Carpe diem!* Seize the day, lads! Make your lives extraordinary!'

As Paul concludes his letter to Timothy, he urges him towards something similar: Take hold of the eternal life to which you were called! Take hold of the life that really is life! Fight the good fight! *Carpe diem*! The impression we get of Timothy throughout this letter is that he was a good man, a young man, slightly nervous of the task set before him, perhaps, and prone to the odd stomach upset (5.23), yet fervent in his desire to see the gospel proclaimed. Paul's purpose in writing seems to be to give this 'man of God' the confidence and practical skills to fulfil his vocation and lead the Ephesian church boldly.

Who is your 'Timothy'? Who is the person you might urge towards making their lives extraordinary? You might not need to write an epistle as Paul did, but there may be other ways – an email, a phone-call, a chat over a cup of tea – of encouraging someone else to go on fighting the good fight.

COLLECT

Almighty God,
in whose service lies perfect freedom:
teach us to obey you
with loving hearts and steadfast wills;
through Jesus Christ our Lord.

Ordinary Time

Wednesday 15 October

Psalm 119.1-32
Leviticus 8
2 Timothy 1.1-14

2 Timothy 1.1-14

Some years later (we are not sure exactly how many), Paul begins a second letter to his dear friend Timothy. Circumstances have changed for Paul, who is now in prison for preaching the gospel. And, from his cell, he urges Timothy not to be ashamed, which, in one sense, Timothy has every right to be. In a culture highly concerned with codes of shame and honour, associating with a political prisoner (as Paul was) carried a high degree of shamefulness. In contrast, Paul encourages Timothy to take a firm stand: 'rekindle the gift', 'hold to ... sound teaching' and 'guard the good treasure' of the gospel.

The basis of Paul's assurance is that he knows the one in whom he trusts, namely Jesus Christ. When I am tempted to be ashamed of the gospel – when I read in the news about Christians doing and saying things that I fear may be misinterpreted by wider society or when I struggle to express coherently the apparent ambiguities of the biblical values to my friends, or even when the hairdresser simply asks me what I do for a living and I mumble something about being a priest – these are the times I too must trust not in who I am or what I do, but in him – Jesus – who is able to forgive my awkwardness and even replace it with confidence.

COLLECT

Grant, we beseech you, merciful Lord,
to your faithful people pardon and peace,
that they may be cleansed from all their sins
and serve you with a quiet mind;
through Jesus Christ your Son our Lord,
who is alive and reigns with you,
in the unity of the Holy Spirit,
one God, now and for ever.

Ordinary Time

Psalms 14, **15**, 16
Leviticus 9
2 Timothy 1.15 – 2.13

Thursday 16 October

2 Timothy 1.15 – 2.13

Perhaps we tend to romanticize the images Paul uses in this passage: gallant, sword-fighting Roman soldiers, discus-throwing Olympians in white togas, jolly farmers straight out of children's Bible story books. Try bringing the images up to date: soldiers in army fatigues battling in Iraq or Afghanistan, track and field athletes training for the Olympics, endeavouring to hold out against performance-enhancing drugs, farmers struggling to make a decent living despite the restrictions of foot-and-mouth or bird flu. What does the allegory for the Christian life look like then? Somewhat less appealing, I expect!

What Paul tries to bring home to Timothy is that there is a great need to 'be strong in grace'. Being a Christian in this age, as in Paul's, is no soft option. It involves battle, discipline and sheer gutsy hard work. Sometimes it's hard to see the good news in what Paul says to Timothy. But it is there. Such determination and endurance will be honoured both in this life and with 'eternal glory' in the next.

And, if we fail to live up to Paul's high standards, Christ is still faithful. That's good news!

> Almighty God,
> in whose service lies perfect freedom:
> teach us to obey you
> with loving hearts and steadfast wills;
> through Jesus Christ our Lord.

COLLECT

Ordinary Time

Friday 17 October

Psalms 17, **19**
Leviticus 16.2-24
2 Timothy 2.14-end

2 Timothy 2.14-end

There is, on the wall of the theological college where I trained, a stone plaque bearing one translation of 2 Timothy verse 15: 'Study to show thyself approved unto God.' That inscription bothered me every time I passed it. Was that what all this study was all about – somehow proving myself to God? Surely he loved me unconditionally. Why did I have to write essays to demonstrate it?

Later, I learned that that particular translation comes from the King James Version. In the seventeenth century, when it was translated, 'study' meant 'be diligent' or 'do your best'. I also found out that the Greek word used for 'show' or 'present' is the same as that used of workers or soldiers turning up for duty, offering themselves to do a task. So, verse 15 more accurately suggests that, knowing ourselves to be already approved by God, we present ourselves wholeheartedly in his service.

No wonder Paul urges Timothy (again) not to be ashamed. His confidence must spring from the knowledge that his identity is not in academic achievements (as I first thought), or in anything else, but in the assurance that God knows and loves all who offer themselves completely to do his work. Far more encouraging than the plaque in my college is God's 'firm foundation' bearing the inscription 'The Lord knows those who are his' (v.19).

COLLECT

Grant, we beseech you, merciful Lord,
to your faithful people pardon and peace,
that they may be cleansed from all their sins
and serve you with a quiet mind;
through Jesus Christ your Son our Lord,
who is alive and reigns with you,
in the unity of the Holy Spirit,
one God, now and for ever.

Ordinary Time

Psalms 145, 146
Isaiah 55
Luke 1.1-4

Saturday 18 October

Luke the Evangelist

Luke 1.1-4

Luke, a doctor and travelling companion of St Paul, wrote both Luke's Gospel and the Acts of the Apostles, which makes him responsible for more of the New Testament than any other writer, including St Paul himself.

Luke's is a voice worth listening to. Not only is his quantity of writing significant but also its quality, its rationale. Luke wrote so that we might 'know the truth'. Fifty years had passed since the death of Christ, and Luke wanted to set down on paper a meticulous account of what Jesus and his followers did, thus passing on the faith to new Christians. Perhaps it is Luke's medical background that causes him to be so concerned that his work is thoroughly investigated and 'orderly'.

Who was Luke writing to? Some say Theophilus was Luke's lawyer, some say a converted Roman official, some say a Jew from Alexandria. 'Theophilus' means 'friend of God' in Greek – so, whoever he was in history, his name might encompass all those who read Luke's Gospel in order to discover a deeper friendship with Christ. Surely Luke would count his work successful if, having read his account, our diagnosis is that Jesus Christ truly is the Son of God who comes to bring life and health to everyone.

COLLECT

Almighty God,
you called Luke the physician,
whose praise is in the gospel,
to be an evangelist and physician of the soul:
by the grace of the Spirit
and through the wholesome medicine of the gospel,
give your Church the same love and power to heal;
through Jesus Christ your Son our Lord,
who is alive and reigns with you,
in the unity of the Holy Spirit,
one God, now and for ever.

Ordinary Time

Monday 20 October

Psalms 27, **30**
Leviticus 19.1-18,30-end
2 Timothy 4.1-8

2 Timothy 4.1-8

It sometimes takes the clarity of someone near the end of their life to see what really matters. It's a matter of debate whether this letter was actually written by Paul. But its author, imprisoned and awaiting execution, writes with considerable urgency in his tone. Throughout the letter, he writes about various issues with a sharp focus on what really matters, and in these verses he simply urges Timothy not to be swayed from what is most important: to keep the faith and proclaim the good news.

'Keep the faith' seems to have two meanings. First, don't give up in the face of opposition or difficulty. Facing execution, if the author had been unsure of his own faith, he would surely have said, 'get out now while you still can'. But even in such extremes, he urges Timothy to persevere. Secondly, there's the sense of preserving the faith. We need to be flexible and imaginative enough to allow the gospel to be embedded in different cultures and successive generations. But we must do so with great care that we are maintaining the same faith, rather than hearing what we want to hear.

So, don't give up because the going gets tough; don't lose sight of what matters; and don't water it down with weak substitutes or mere ear-tickling ideas. Keep the faith.

COLLECT

Almighty God,
who alone can bring order
to the unruly wills and passions of sinful humanity:
give your people grace
so to love what you command
and to desire what you promise,
that, among the many changes of this world,
our hearts may surely there be fixed
where true joys are to be found;
through Jesus Christ your Son our Lord,
who is alive and reigns with you,
in the unity of the Holy Spirit,
one God, now and for ever.

Ordinary Time

Psalms 32, **36**
Leviticus 23.1-22
2 Timothy 4.9-end

Tuesday 21 October

2 Timothy 4.9-end

The last few years have seen all too much news coverage of people being taken hostage. Cruelly shot video footage has shown the violent end of some victims; others survive and write books afterwards. In these ways, we've caught glimpses of the extreme pressure undergone by people who are imprisoned, isolated and in fear of their lives, because of a clash of cultures or political and religious causes.

The writer of 2 Timothy was similarly in extreme circumstances, feeling acutely the need for human contact, yet also experiencing a mental anguish common among hostages – the fear that he had been abandoned. Twice he refers to people who had 'deserted' him, despite the fact that Luke was with him and that he was relaying messages from a supportive community.

In such circumstances, even the strongest person becomes vulnerable. Let us never forget or abandon those who are now imprisoned for their religious and political beliefs. But, at the same time, let's learn from this that spiritual leaders don't have to be superheroes. We are merely called to be saints, despite our vulnerability, despite the failings that come to minds wearied by anxiety and pressure. In the words of Oscar Romero, himself martyred for the faith in 1980, 'we are ministers, not messiahs'.

COLLECT

Eternal God,
whose Son went among the crowds
and brought healing with his touch:
help us to show his love,
in your Church as we gather together,
and by our lives as they are transformed
into the image of Christ our Lord.

Ordinary Time

Wednesday 22 October

Psalm **34**
Leviticus 23.23-end
Titus 1

Titus 1

The New Testament writers all struggled to express a right balance between faith and works. The letter to Titus opens with an emphasis on good works and self-discipline, but later clearly places this within salvation and holiness as gifts from God.

The author begins by urging Titus to be 'blameless', which to a twenty-first-century reader could sound somewhat holier-than-thou. But this is far from a rule-book approach to self-discipline. Rather, it has an undercurrent of freedom to it, concerned with getting underlying attitudes right. 'To the pure,' he says, 'all things are pure' – the point is not stringent self-denial, but ordering our lives in a way that is congruent with the God we know. The author's standards are strict, yet there is a warmth to his instructions to Titus to be hospitable and a lover of goodness. Food, drink, entertainments, relationships – none of these is denied us; the point is that they are good or bad depending upon the attitude of heart with which we approach them.

In criticizing those 'who profess to know God, but ... deny him by their actions', then, he is not falling into a 'salvation by works', but affirming an integrity of life where faith and works are of a piece. As a result, we develop sound judgement, so that a rule-book approach to holiness is unnecessary, and the practical and the spiritual are not divided.

COLLECT

Almighty God,
who alone can bring order
to the unruly wills and passions of sinful humanity:
give your people grace
so to love what you command
and to desire what you promise,
that, among the many changes of this world,
our hearts may surely there be fixed
where true joys are to be found;
through Jesus Christ your Son our Lord,
who is alive and reigns with you,
in the unity of the Holy Spirit,
one God, now and for ever.

Ordinary Time

Psalm 37*
Leviticus 24.1-9
Titus 2

Thursday 23 October

Titus 2

The writer urges Titus to teach 'what is consistent with sound doctrine' – not speaking here of doctrine itself, but a lifestyle characteristic of a community professing Christian faith. He distinguishes between spiritual aspirations for older and younger people. It's thought that Titus himself was a young man, so the words 'Let no one look down on you' are an encouragement to him not to let his confidence be undermined because of his youth.

Even now, people use either age or youth as an excuse to dismiss one another's ministries. Older people sometimes assume that the young know nothing, whereas young people can dismiss the middle-aged and the elderly as being out of date. This letter to Titus calls us to remember that people of all ages have their contribution to make. Mutual respect for each other's faith and ministry should characterize a Christian community. But, more than that, Paul encourages relationship across the generations, a genuine exchange of wisdom and friendship between old and young, slave and free.

Some current ideas of the future of the Church overlook this cross-pollination. For us, it means we must still discover that the Body of Christ only flourishes when there is genuine inclusion and interaction across cultural divisions of age and race, gender and class.

> Eternal God,
> whose Son went among the crowds
> and brought healing with his touch:
> help us to show his love,
> in your Church as we gather together,
> and by our lives as they are transformed
> into the image of Christ our Lord.

COLLECT

Ordinary Time

Friday 24 October

Psalm 31
Leviticus 25.1-24
Titus 3

Titus 3

In this final chapter, the writer continues his call to godly living. But the foundational assumption of the letter is reinforced – that our efforts in personal morality and good works do not in themselves make us godly. Their value is as a response to the gift of God's salvation and imputed spirit. As we saw earlier, the author clearly places good works as a response to salvation. Deliberate acts of faith do not earn God's gifts, but make it possible for the ongoing, transforming work of the indwelling Spirit to take place. Again, behind the strict tone we see a warmth here: we are reminded that salvation is an act of God's kindness, not reproof. Holiness, then, is not merely an exercise in stringent constraint. We are saved not because God disapproves of us, but because God loves us.

There's an interesting juxtaposition in this chapter between the call to be peaceable and obedient, and the warning to reject those who are factious. A good reminder, perhaps, that being peaceable doesn't mean being spineless or having no opinions – it means being wise, determined and alert, and not allowing others to destroy the pursuit of peace. The writer's warning to avoid foolish controversies transfers across the centuries with absolute clarity. When disputes over side issues become the central focus of our faith, they destroy our own peace and our proclamation of the gospel.

COLLECT

Almighty God,
who alone can bring order
to the unruly wills and passions of sinful humanity:
give your people grace
so to love what you command
and to desire what you promise,
that, among the many changes of this world,
our hearts may surely there be fixed
where true joys are to be found;
through Jesus Christ your Son our Lord,
who is alive and reigns with you,
in the unity of the Holy Spirit,
one God, now and for ever.

Ordinary Time

Psalms 41, **42**, 43
Numbers 6.1-5,21-end
Philemon

Saturday 25 October

Philemon

What is the purpose of including this very brief letter in the New Testament?

Despite being addressed to three people and a whole church, from verse 4 onwards, 'you' is in the singular. So, it's really a letter to one person, Philemon, about the welfare of just one person, Onesimus. It isn't clear why Onesimus left Philemon's service, but it appears that the two men fell out over some issue. Paul pleads with Philemon to bury the hatchet and take Onesimus back, as a brother, not a slave.

Although this personal letter gives us little doctrinal material, then, it does demonstrate the care taken by the early Church missionaries, both in the care and welfare of their individual disciples and in the restoration of broken relationships. For these early missionaries, to belong to the Church meant forging relationships, not just for their own sake, but because the Church couldn't survive if its members were divided from one another. Even established social divisions such as slave and master were broken down in the Church. For us, too, we must not allow differences in class, race, age, gender or sexuality to separate us from our brothers and sisters in Christ.

COLLECT

Eternal God,
whose Son went among the crowds
and brought healing with his touch:
help us to show his love,
in your Church as we gather together,
and by our lives as they are transformed
into the image of Christ our Lord.

Ordinary Time

Monday 27 October

Psalm **44**
Genesis 18.1-15
Matthew 27.11-26

Genesis 18.1-15

Hospitality in nomadic cultures is not a matter of politeness or generosity, but a matter of life and death, as another source of food, water and shelter might be many hours' travel away. When three men approached Abram's settlement, it appears that at first he did not recognize them as out of the ordinary. His offer of hospitality was not unusual, motivated by his recognition of a visit from angels, but was simply what he would extend to any stranger passing through. This is where the phrase 'angels unawares' comes from. It seems that it only gradually dawns on Abram and Sarai that their guests are no ordinary men – and, by the end of the chapter, Abram is talking to one of them openly as 'the Lord'.

From the point of view of Christian theology, an important thread in this story is that there is the potential to encounter something of God in the face and presence of any person who comes across our path, simply because we believe that every person is made in the image of God. In this sense, we, too, might entertain 'angels' unawares – for, in the words of Christ, 'just as you did it to one of the least of these who are members of my family, you did it to me' (Matthew 25.40).

COLLECT

Blessed Lord,
who caused all holy Scriptures to be written for our learning:
help us so to hear them,
to read, mark, learn and inwardly digest them
that, through patience, and the comfort of your holy word,
we may embrace and for ever hold fast
    the hope of everlasting life,
which you have given us in our Saviour Jesus Christ,
who is alive and reigns with you,
in the unity of the Holy Spirit,
one God, now and for ever.

Ordinary Time

Psalms 116, 117
Isaiah 45.18-end
Luke 6.12-16

Tuesday 28 October

Simon and Jude, Apostles

Luke 6.12-16

Simon the Zealot and Jude are only mentioned by name in the New Testament in these lists of the apostles. Ancient Christian sources suggest that Simon and Jude went to Persia together as missionaries, where they were martyred, which could explain why we have very little information about them and why they are celebrated together.

The original Greek 'Judas of James' may be translated as the son of James, or the brother of James. So, he could have been the brother of the ninth disciple, James son of Alphaeus. Alternatively, he could have been the author of the Epistle of Jude, who is also listed as the brother of James. On the feast of Simon and Jude, we celebrate both Judes – Jude the son or brother of James, and Jude the author of the Epistle – without any clarity as to whether the last two were in fact the same person.

Perhaps their inclusion in the list of apostles without any further history is a good reminder to us, in a culture obsessed with celebrities, that our significance in the kingdom of God is not attached to fame or glory. Appointed from among hundreds of followers of Jesus to carry out special tasks, they were only minimally and vaguely remembered by history. But their significance as people and the gifts they brought to the proclamation of the gospel were noticed and affirmed by Jesus.

> Almighty God,
> who built your Church upon the foundation
> of the apostles and prophets,
> with Jesus Christ himself as the chief cornerstone:
> so join us together in unity of spirit by their doctrine,
> that we may be made a holy temple acceptable to you;
> through Jesus Christ your Son our Lord,
> who is alive and reigns with you,
> in the unity of the Holy Spirit,
> one God, now and for ever.

COLLECT

Ordinary Time

Wednesday 29 October

Psalm 119.57-80
Genesis 19.1-3,12-29
Matthew 27.45-56

Genesis 19.1-3,12-29

Stories such as this present no problem to us if we read them simply as ancient myths. But if, within these pages, we seek a God to believe in today, it's highly problematic to encounter a God who rains down volcanic fire in judgement on a city. Natural disasters were once attributed directly to 'the gods'; now that they are not, what can we draw from Lot's story?

What strikes me is how reluctant the main players were to be saved from disaster. Lot's sons-in-law were entirely unconvinced when Lot told them to flee the city – perhaps unsurprisingly, since Lot himself didn't have any sense of urgency and lingered in Sodom. Eventually, the angels grabbed Lot, his wife and his daughters by the hand and led them out of the city – even then, Lot was slow to get moving.

Lot is saved by God's repeated acts of mercy. God not only offers Lot a way of escape, but quite literally grabs him by the hand and saves him, despite his own inability to grasp the reality of his situation. The mercy of God is a deliberate act of salvation – not in the sense that Lot is saved against his own will, but in the sense that the kindness of God does not depend on us if we have no will or energy to save ourselves.

COLLECT

Blessed Lord,
who caused all holy Scriptures to be written for our learning:
help us so to hear them,
to read, mark, learn and inwardly digest them
that, through patience, and the comfort of your holy word,
we may embrace and for ever hold fast
    the hope of everlasting life,
which you have given us in our Saviour Jesus Christ,
who is alive and reigns with you,
in the unity of the Holy Spirit,
one God, now and for ever.

Ordinary Time

Psalms 56, **57** (63*)
Genesis 21.1-21
Matthew 27.57-end

Thursday 30 October

Genesis 21.1-21

For many people reading the Patriarchal narratives, one thing that jars is precisely that they are patriarchal and often reinforce outdated stereotypes about women, children, immigrants or people of other faiths. But here we see women, children and foreigners becoming the direct recipients of the blessings originally promised only to Abraham.

God's covenant is expanded to include Sarah in Genesis 17.16: 'I will bless her and she shall give rise to nations.' And, when Sarah callously sends Ishmael and Hagar out into the desert to die, God refuses to write off Ishmael as a mistake, and again extends his promise that Ishmael, too, will be fruitful and a father of nations.

It would be extravagant to claim that this amounts to 'women and children first'! But, although this may not be a twenty-first-century account of equality and justice, still the women are not written out of the story, nor the unwanted children dismissed without a care. Amid these complicated accounts, there is enough honest reality, and enough of the ends left untied, for us to see through the gaps in the stories to a God whose justice, fairness and love prevails despite the inequities of an ancient and sometimes brutal patriarchal culture. And here the beginning of the salvation story prefigures its eventual fulfilment when a child and a woman, in a patriarchal society, become the embodiment of God's blessing and promise.

> Merciful God,
> teach us to be faithful in change and uncertainty,
> that trusting in your word
> and obeying your will
> we may enter the unfailing joy of Jesus Christ our Lord.

COLLECT

Ordinary Time

Friday 31 October

Psalms **51**, 54
Genesis 22.1-19
Matthew 28.1-15

Genesis 22.1-19

It's thought that child-sacrifice was a common religious practice in Abraham's time and culture. So, this story can be read as an illustration of the way we absorb cultural assumptions and then project them onto God. 'Sacrifice is what religion is all about, ergo God wants me to make painful sacrifices.' It's only over time that we recognize that these are our own assumptions, and can allow our view of God to be changed. In Abraham's case, he eventually discovered that the appalling spectre of child-sacrifice was not within the kindness of his God.

Traditionally, parallels have been made between this story and the sacrifice made by Jesus. But it also might speak to us of the need for discernment in the sacrifices we expect ourselves and others to make in the name of God, over matters of religious principle. True love of any kind, whether for God or for other people, always demands sacrifices. What's difficult is to discern when we are genuinely called to make sacrifices for a principle or a cause, and when it's time to walk in another direction – perhaps to walk away from a destructive workplace or marriage or church community. This story teaches us that there are humane limits to what God demands from us in terms of sacrifice. The destructive abuse of another human being is never within the scheme of God.

COLLECT

Blessed Lord,
who caused all holy Scriptures to be written for our learning:
help us so to hear them,
to read, mark, learn and inwardly digest them
that, through patience, and the comfort of your holy word,
we may embrace and for ever hold fast
    the hope of everlasting life,
which you have given us in our Saviour Jesus Christ,
who is alive and reigns with you,
in the unity of the Holy Spirit,
one God, now and for ever.

Ordinary Time

Psalms 15, 84, 149
Isaiah 35
Luke 9.18-27

Saturday 1 November

All Saints' Day

Luke 9.18-27

Jesus' questions to his disciples are intriguing. By asking first 'Who do the crowds say that I am?' and then 'But who do *you* say that I am?', was Jesus trying to work something out for himself? Or was he trying to make them decide what they thought? It's easy for us to assume that Jesus of Nazareth shared God's omniscience. Yet there are plenty of signs that he may only gradually have developed his sense of identity as God's son.

As Luke tells it, Peter's confession of faith is immediately followed by Jesus' prediction of his own death and resurrection, and then his call to the crowds to decide whether or not to follow him on this sombre journey.

All the followers of Jesus, right back through history, are remembered on All Saints' Day. All of them, and all of us, have this in common – that we recognize Jesus as the Son of God, and we decide that, whatever road it takes us down, we believe in him enough to want to follow him wherever that belief leads us. The saints are not only those who are painted in stained glass or revered in ancient churches, but all the followers of Jesus, whether they are remembered by name, like Peter, or are just one of the crowd.

COLLECT

Almighty God,
you have knit together your elect
in one communion and fellowship
in the mystical body of your Son Christ our Lord:
grant us grace so to follow your blessed saints
in all virtuous and godly living
that we may come to those inexpressible joys
that you have prepared for those who truly love you;
through Jesus Christ your Son our Lord,
who is alive and reigns with you,
in the unity of the Holy Spirit,
one God, now and for ever.

Ordinary Time: All Saints to Advent

Monday 3 November

Psalms **2**, 146 or **71**
Daniel 1
Revelation 1

Revelation 1

It is sometimes suggested that Revelation was written under the influence of mind-altering drugs. Perhaps, however, Revelation itself is the mind-altering substance, one designed to overturn our earthbound perceptions.

Take, for example, our understanding of the relationship between the Church and the godhead. John sees the churches as seven lampstands. Note that they are lampstands and not lamps. Why are the churches described as inanimate objects? What role can they have in a story where other characters are all fire, action and light?

The relationship between the divine and the mundane is revealed in the lamp-lighting drama that follows. Christ holds seven stars in his right hand. He places this hand on John's head and commands him to write to the seven churches. Could it be that Christ is sending the seven stars to serve as flames for the each of the lampstands? We are told that these stars are the angels of the seven churches (1.20), and there is an intriguing possibility that they also represent the Holy Spirit which, in seven parts, is sent out into all the earth (4.5; 5.6). As the inanimate lampstands are set alight by the stars, so the Church is animated by the Spirit.

COLLECT

Almighty and eternal God,
you have kindled the flame of love
    in the hearts of the saints:
grant to us the same faith and power of love,
that, as we rejoice in their triumphs,
we may be sustained by their example and fellowship;
through Jesus Christ your Son our Lord,
who is alive and reigns with you,
in the unity of the Holy Spirit,
one God, now and for ever.

Ordinary Time: All Saints to Advent

Psalms **5**, 147.1-12 *or* **77**
Daniel 2.1-24
Revelation 2.1-11

Tuesday 4 November

Revelation 2.1-11

What is the goal? It is easy enough for our churches, like the church at Ephesus, to equate the fulfilment of our purpose with the achievement of doctrinal correctness. The Ephesians were vigilant on every side, against evildoers, false apostles and Nicolaitans. They were dogged in their determination to bear up under pressure and steadfastly to profess the true faith. All these qualities are treated as positives in Christ's assessment of the church – and yet, in spite of all his commendations, they also receive an extraordinary reprimand. Christ threatens to remove their lampstand from its place. What, amid all their correctness, could they be getting so wrong? It is not clear whether it is the love of God or of neighbour that has become their blind spot, but the intimate relationship between the two suggests that it may be both. Right doctrine is a means to an end, not an end in itself.

Perceptions are also shifted in Smyrna. That which is being forced out of existence by economic, religious and political pressures is, as Revelation would have us see it, in the process of being born to eternal life. How we see ourselves, and how God sees us, may fall at opposite ends of a single spectrum.

> God of glory,
> touch our lips with the fire of your Spirit,
> that we with all creation
> may rejoice to sing your praise;
> through Jesus Christ our Lord.

COLLECT

Ordinary Time: All Saints to Advent

Wednesday 5 November

Psalms **9**, 147.13-end *or* **77**
Daniel 2.25-end
Revelation 2.12-end

Revelation 2.12-end

Like a cartoonist, Revelation depicts personalities in its original readers' everyday life in guises designed to reveal their true character. 'Balaam' and 'Jezebel' are evidently held in high standing by at least some of the congregation at Pergamum and Thyatira. By giving them these loaded nicknames, however, the readers are invited to view respected figures in a more circumspect light. Are they really prophets of Jesus Christ, or are they governed by an alternative set of interests?

The references to adultery and eating food offered to idols indicate that these teachers were encouraging Christians to compromise the exclusivity of their allegiance to Christ. This would have been a very attractive message in a world where the ability to trade and participate in public life would have required a certain willingness to slip in and out of different allegiances. This is an issue, however, where Revelation is completely inflexible. To eat at the table of Christ, at the Eucharist, is to indicate membership of the body of Christ. To eat at another table is fundamentally to violate that membership. Soft words of compromise are as attractive now as they ever were, but Revelation warns that such paths may lead to a thoroughly destructive destination.

COLLECT

Almighty and eternal God,
you have kindled the flame of love
   in the hearts of the saints:
grant to us the same faith and power of love,
that, as we rejoice in their triumphs,
we may be sustained by their example and fellowship;
through Jesus Christ your Son our Lord,
who is alive and reigns with you,
in the unity of the Holy Spirit,
one God, now and for ever.

Ordinary Time: All Saints to Advent

Psalms 11, **15**, 148 *or* **78.1-39***
Daniel 3.1-18
Revelation 3.1-13

Thursday 6 November

Revelation 3.1-13

Five of the seven letters to the churches begin with the phrase 'I know your works'. When it comes to Christ's assessment of the deep truth about each church, it seems that actions are the favoured measure of reality. Even here, however, there is a risk that 'works' form part of an individual church's public-relations campaign, designed to manipulate impressions and win warm words from the neighbouring community. The works that Christ is interested in here are those designed to impress an audience of one, and are often those which go unnoticed, or are even opposed, by others.

The churches at Sardis and Philadelphia are good examples of the potentially inverse relationship between reputation and reality. Sardis appears strong but is close to death; Philadelphia appears powerless but is promised a permanent place in God's intimate company. There is a particularly touching pastoral sensitivity in Christ's response to the Philadelphians' situation. They are excluded and despised by their more powerful neighbours, but are assured of a very different reception by God himself. His door is always open; their place in his company is a permanent fixture. The name of God, the name of Christ and their heavenly address is inscribed upon them as an indelible declaration of their preciousness in God's estimation.

> God of glory,
> touch our lips with the fire of your Spirit,
> that we with all creation
> may rejoice to sing your praise;
> through Jesus Christ our Lord.

COLLECT

Ordinary Time: All Saints to Advent

Friday 7 November

Psalms **16**, 149 *or* **55**
Daniel 3.19-end
Revelation 3.14-end

Revelation 3.14-end

The path of least resistance is, by definition, always the hardest to resist. The Laodicean Christians found themselves in a situation where, with a few compromises here and there, they could live a comfortable, prosperous life while continuing to practise their faith. At least, that was how they saw things. Revelation's view, on the other hand, is somewhat different. To mix allegiance to Christ with allegiance to any other entity, it argues, is like mixing pure, refreshing drinking water with hot bath water. The result is undrinkable. If it is riches that we are interested in, Revelation advises, we should acquire 'gold refined by fire' – a reference to faith proven under persecution. Similarly, if we want real clothes, we should seek 'white robes', which represent blameless behaviour. The easy self-satisfaction of the Laodicean church is perhaps more reminiscent of the Western churches of today than any of the other seven churches. A Christ's-eye view of our church may be similarly challenging.

Despite the consistent distaste expressed in this letter, Christ persists in offering an invitation to eat with him. The meal in question is most likely the Eucharist, participation in which provides an opportunity to reaffirm, and delight in, membership in Christ alone.

COLLECT

Almighty and eternal God,
you have kindled the flame of love
   in the hearts of the saints:
grant to us the same faith and power of love,
that, as we rejoice in their triumphs,
we may be sustained by their example and fellowship;
through Jesus Christ your Son our Lord,
who is alive and reigns with you,
in the unity of the Holy Spirit,
one God, now and for ever.

Ordinary Time: All Saints to Advent

Psalms **18.31-end**, 150 *or* **76**, 79
Daniel 4.1-18
Revelation 4

Saturday 8 November

Revelation 4

Revelation is commonly understood as a text which seeks to predict the future. Another way of looking at it, however, is to see it as a revelation of the totality of the present; a present from which certain future consequences must necessarily flow. Essential to Revelation's depiction of the present is the throne scene of chapter 4. The layers of symbolism in this chapter emphasize the complete sovereignty of God over all the universe. First, the throne itself is a symbol of power, and the tangential description of the one seated on the throne serves to emphasize his otherness. The significance of the 24 thrones is not immediately clear, but it is possible that they symbolize the hours of the day and God's sovereignty over time. The four living creatures represent four dimensions of the created order – wild animals, domestic animals, humans and birds – and show how all creation is orientated in worship of the one on the throne.

The message that emanates from this vision is that of the almightiness of God. Some extraordinarily challenging and painful episodes will be depicted in the remainder of the text, but this vision provides an overarching canopy for them all. There is no event, no matter how terrible, that can evade, dislodge or undermine the ultimate power of God.

God of glory,
touch our lips with the fire of your Spirit,
that we with all creation
may rejoice to sing your praise;
through Jesus Christ our Lord.

COLLECT

Ordinary Time: All Saints to Advent

Monday 10 November

Psalms 19, **20** *or* 80, 82
Daniel 4.19-end
Revelation 5

Revelation 5

Together, chapters 4 and 5 form the heart of John's Revelation. This is the larger reality from which every other element of the story flows. If chapter 4 serves to emphasize God's power, then chapter 5 gives us an extraordinary insight into the source of that power: God's vulnerability. It is worth pausing to note that the one who controls the outcome of all history is depicted as a lamb who stands as if he has been slaughtered.

Chapters 4 and 5 build in our imaginations an ever-expanding picture of the whole universe. At the focus of worship and the centre of dramatic tension lies the one on the throne, the Lamb and the scroll. This scroll contains the story of 'what must soon take place', as promised in 1.1, 1.19 and 4.1, the contents of which are eagerly awaited by John and those who long for God's saving justice. Through the course of chapter 5, the camera angle widens to reveal the presence of myriad angels who, like the elders and living creatures, are focused on this central tableau. As the vision expands still further, every creature in heaven and on earth and under the earth is similarly transfixed. The attention of every element of the universe is focused in a particular direction. We are invited to share their gaze and to join in the worship they offer.

COLLECT

Almighty Father,
whose will is to restore all things
in your beloved Son, the King of all:
govern the hearts and minds of those in authority,
and bring the families of the nations,
divided and torn apart by the ravages of sin,
to be subject to his just and gentle rule;
who is alive and reigns with you,
in the unity of the Holy Spirit,
one God, now and for ever.

Ordinary Time: All Saints to Advent

Psalms **21**, 24 *or* 87, **89.1-18**
Daniel 5.1-12
Revelation 6

Tuesday 11 November

Revelation 6

The scroll of ultimate consequence is sealed with seven seals. It would be hard to set up a more suspense-laden scenario. We cannot see the contents of this all-important scroll until all its seals have been broken, but as each seal is removed, an accompanying vision gives us a foretaste of what lies inside. The four riders, one of the best-known images from Revelation, are called out by each of the four living creatures that stand 'around the throne and on each side of the throne' (4.6). They are sent off in four different directions to warn each quadrant of the earth of the judgements soon to be revealed. It is possible that all six visions in this sequence refer to events in the shared history of the original audience – for example, the civil war that followed Nero's suicide in AD 68, the martyrdom of Christians after the burning of Rome in AD 64, and the eruption of Vesuvius in AD 79. If this is the case, then the reader is being invited to observe that what has happened in the past is a sign of what is likely to happen in the future, only more so. In our own times, we have experienced terrible wars, persecutions and natural disasters. We need to be prepared for the recurrence of such events; they are not relics of another age.

God, our refuge and strength,
bring near the day when wars shall cease
and poverty and pain shall end,
that earth may know the peace of heaven
through Jesus Christ our Lord.

COLLECT

Ordinary Time: All Saints to Advent

Wednesday 12 November

Psalms **23**, 25 *or* **119.105-128**
Daniel 5.13-end
Revelation 7.1-4,9-end

Revelation 7.1-4,9-end

The scroll that promises to unleash the final judgements is now held shut by one seal only. The tension is unbearable. Is there any cause for hope? Is there any differentiation between the just and the unjust in all that is about to take place?

Then, the pause button is hit. All is still; no wind blows. An angel intervenes to equip the saints with a means of surviving – in a spiritual and eternal sense, if not in an immediate and physical one – the juggernaut of disaster that hurtles through chapter 6. The protective seal they receive is perhaps a reference to Holy Baptism.

Those who are thus sealed are presented in 'before' and 'after' pictures. In the 'before' picture, they are characterized as the true Israel, a franchise strongly contested by John's opponents (cf. 2.9; 3.9). In the 'after' picture, the same group is shown to have survived all that is to come, safely arriving to enjoy the eternal and intimate company of God. In the course of their trials, this group is swelled to an innumerable crowd from every tribe, tongue, people and nation. All baptized believers have a place among this crowd; it is the unshakable destination of every faithful Christian life.

COLLECT

Almighty Father,
whose will is to restore all things
in your beloved Son, the King of all:
govern the hearts and minds of those in authority,
and bring the families of the nations,
divided and torn apart by the ravages of sin,
to be subject to his just and gentle rule;
who is alive and reigns with you,
in the unity of the Holy Spirit,
one God, now and for ever.

Ordinary Time: All Saints to Advent

Psalms **26**, 27 *or* 90, **92**
Daniel 6
Revelation 8

Thursday 13 November

Revelation 8

The last remaining seal is broken. Surely now the contents of the scroll will be unleashed to do their terrible work? It seems not. First of all, there is silence in heaven for 'about half an hour'. The purpose of this pause is not spelled out, but if the text was designed to be experienced in a worship setting, then the earthly audience may well have taken this hiatus as an opportunity to cry out to God for justice and salvation. This is one of several occasions when Revelation reminds its earthly hearers that we are active participants, and not mere passive observers, in the cosmic drama.

Like the visions that accompanied the breaking of each seal in chapter 6, the trumpet visions dramatically announce what will take place once the great scroll's contents are finally made known (cf. 10.7). Once again, it is possible that the original readers were being invited to interpret real events as somehow signalling an escalated cycle of similar events in the future (cf. 16.2-8). Revelation's message for our own age might be to encourage us to observe the present consequences of environmental damage as prefiguring larger and more intense consequences yet to come.

COLLECT

God, our refuge and strength,
bring near the day when wars shall cease
and poverty and pain shall end,
that earth may know the peace of heaven
through Jesus Christ our Lord.

Ordinary Time: All Saints to Advent

Friday 14 November

Psalms 28, **32** *or* 88 (95)
Daniel 7.1-14
Revelation 9.1-12

Revelation 9.1-12

It is easy, particularly in a passage such as this one, to assume that the seer has lost all contact with any version of reality with which we might be familiar. However, it is not the case that historical reality is abandoned in these passages. Instead, as Revelation dances along the boundary between what we know and what we do not yet know, we are being schooled in the art of prophecy; that is to say, the ability to see real historical events through spiritual spectacles.

The eruption of Vesuvius, in AD 79, would provide a fitting historical background to the first two verses of this vision. What is to be made of this unprecedented disaster? Perhaps John is using it as a visual aid, on a grand scale, to depict the great cosmic drama in which Satan, thrown down to earth by Christ's victory, releases the agents by which he will attempt to destroy Christ's followers. By this means, Revelation makes the battle in which we are called to be engaged both vivid and immediate. This battle may be one we would rather minimize and downplay, but Revelation uses every means at its disposal to prevent us from doing so.

COLLECT

Almighty Father,
whose will is to restore all things
in your beloved Son, the King of all:
govern the hearts and minds of those in authority,
and bring the families of the nations,
divided and torn apart by the ravages of sin,
to be subject to his just and gentle rule;
who is alive and reigns with you,
in the unity of the Holy Spirit,
one God, now and for ever.

Ordinary Time: All Saints to Advent

Psalms 33 *or* 96, **97**, 100
Daniel 7.15-end
Revelation 9.13-end

Saturday 15 November

Revelation 9.13-end

The thunder of 200,000,000 sets of hooves threatens to drown out our memory of the context in which this vision is set. The first, and most important, context is the sovereignty of God, established in chapters 4 and 5. There is nothing that takes place in this narrative, or in the history that it reflects, that is not ultimately governed by God's will. It can be difficult for us to reconcile this idea with the horror represented here, but there can be no doubt that Revelation allows the possibility that evil forces may be used for a God-ordained purpose; in this case, as a means of punishment. Later in the narrative, this agent of judgement will itself be subject to God's justice.

A second context is provided by the relationship between all six trumpet-blasts and the prayers of the saints, as set up in 8.3-5. God's action in judgement is presented as a response to these prayers. If we feel discomfort at this idea, then it may help to place ourselves in the situation of those whose only hope, in the face of persecution and martyrdom for their allegiance to Jesus Christ, is to cry out to the God on whom they can rely for true and lasting justice.

> God, our refuge and strength,
> bring near the day when wars shall cease
> and poverty and pain shall end,
> that earth may know the peace of heaven
> through Jesus Christ our Lord.

COLLECT

Ordinary Time: All Saints to Advent

Monday 17 November

Psalms 46, 47 *or* 98, 99, 101
Daniel 8.1-14
Revelation 10

Revelation 10

Why is the world as it is, and what is God doing about it? This is one helpful way to understand what the book of Revelation is about: answering this question for the gathered followers of Jesus, who are under severe pressure – whether they realize it or not.

Just as we reach the climax of the trumpets – as with the seals in chapter 7 – the pause button is hit. Another angel, 'strong' or 'mighty' like the one in 5.2, is described in terms that remind us of the risen Christ, though is clearly distinct from him. He comes to announce further judgement, but the 'voice from heaven' will not allow it. Even though judgement must come, and its first purpose is to turn humanity from false worship (9.20), God himself is a reluctant dispenser of calamity.

Instead, John is commissioned as a new Ezekiel to proclaim God's message. And, like Ezekiel, he finds it a sweet message at first, but one that is hard to swallow in its entirety. The good news of the kingdom brings with it a call to steadfast, faithful witness in the face of suffering. Yet the scope of this message is cosmic – it is not just for John, nor just for those who own Christ now, but it will extend to touch every nation on earth. Such is God's vision for the redemption of his fallen world.

COLLECT

Heavenly Father,
whose blessed Son was revealed
   to destroy the works of the devil
and to make us the children of God and heirs of eternal life:
grant that we, having this hope,
may purify ourselves even as he is pure;
that when he shall appear in power and great glory
we may be made like him in his eternal and glorious kingdom;
where he is alive and reigns with you,
in the unity of the Holy Spirit,
one God, now and for ever.

Ordinary Time: All Saints to Advent

Psalms 48, **52** *or* **106*** (or 103)
Daniel 8.15-end
Revelation 11.1-14

Tuesday 18 November

Revelation 11.1-14

The pause continues. What has not been achieved by natural disasters might yet be brought about by the faithful witness of God's people.

Again echoing Ezekiel (chapter 40), John is given a rod with which to measure the temple. But, instead of measuring an ideal temple in a vision, John is asked to consider those who worship the true God in the present. On outward appearance, these worshippers look as though they are suffering the three and a half years (42 months) of desolation predicted by Daniel. But the inner reality is that they are kept safe – the power to witness lasts 1,260 days, which is 42 months of 30 days each.

And God's people are kept safe for a purpose. We are to witness, fulfilling the biblical injunction of two witnesses in agreement. We are to be the first fruits of the return from the exile of sin, just as were Zerubbabel and Joshua as they re-established the worship of God in the land. As we exercise the prophetic ministries of Elijah (shutting the sky) and Moses (bringing plagues), in human terms we continually face defeat; our message really is too much for the peoples to stomach. But God's resurrection life in us will astonish our persecutors; those who receive it as a message of life and not death will, in the end, see the truth and give glory to God.

COLLECT

Heavenly Lord,
you long for the world's salvation:
stir us from apathy,
restrain us from excess
and revive in us new hope
that all creation will one day be healed
in Jesus Christ our Lord.

Ordinary Time: All Saints to Advent

Wednesday 19 November

Psalms **56**, 57 *or* 110, **111**, 112
Daniel 9.1-19
Revelation 11.15-end

Revelation 11.15-end

The pause button of chapters 10 and 11 is released, and the action resumes. We finally come to the seventh trumpet, which, within this series of sevens, ushers in the end of the world. With each series, we begin to get a clearer picture of what the world is like and what its end means. The final seal (8.1) brought a response of silence and prayer; the final trumpet gives way to a response of celebration and worship.

'Loud voices' (v.15) proclaim that the kingdom (or 'empire') of this world is now transformed into the anticipated kingdom of God brought about by the work of his Messiah. Unlike all human pretensions to lasting significance, this kingdom really will be enduring. The elders, who in chapter 4 worshipped the one who 'is to come', now experience his presence in blessing and judgement, and see how he has brought to an end all the forces of destruction in the world (v.18).

Our worship can at times feel mundane and fleeting. And yet it should ring with the same confidence and anticipation. Our approaches to God, on our own day by day and with others week by week, find their fulfilment in this future. We are those elders, falling down in the face of ultimate reality, participating in the only thing that will truly endure.

COLLECT

Heavenly Father,
whose blessed Son was revealed
    to destroy the works of the devil
and to make us the children of God and heirs of eternal life:
grant that we, having this hope,
may purify ourselves even as he is pure;
that when he shall appear in power and great glory
we may be made like him in his eternal and glorious kingdom;
where he is alive and reigns with you,
in the unity of the Holy Spirit,
one God, now and for ever.

Ordinary Time: All Saints to Advent

Psalms 61, **62** *or* 113, **115**
Daniel 9.20-end
Revelation 12

Thursday 20 November

Revelation 12

With the resurgence of vocal atheism, the challenge of other faiths, continued questioning of traditional morality and ever-faster changes in technology, we can sometimes feel as though we are being drawn into a trial of strength with the cultural forces of our day. Only those who are strong enough will survive, let alone prosper.

Yet in this passage we see layer upon layer of weakness and vulnerability as the means of God's power and victory. God's expectant people are depicted, using imagery from Isaiah 66 and Micah 3, as a woman in the very pains of labour (v.2) – you could hardly find an image of greater vulnerability. Then the promise of God's deliverance of his people takes the form of a child (v.5), snatched away to safety with unseemly haste. And the victory is celebrated (v.11) by those who have nothing more powerful to offer than words of testimony and who have, like the Lamb, paid the price of faithfulness to the point of death. And yet victory it is.

It is as we offer our weakness and vulnerability that God's power and victory breaks through. Just as the decisive victory over the Accuser was won through weakness, so we live in that victory as we offer our weaknesses and allow God the space to do his work. Perhaps, then, the most important question is not 'Why am I weak?' but 'Where am I weak?' This is the place where God's victory will be revealed; this is the place where we can stand in the power that God alone can provide.

COLLECT

Heavenly Lord,
you long for the world's salvation:
stir us from apathy,
restrain us from excess
and revive in us new hope
that all creation will one day be healed
in Jesus Christ our Lord.

Ordinary Time: All Saints to Advent

Friday 21 November

Psalms **63**, 65 *or* **139**
Daniel 10.1 – 11.1
Revelation 13.1-10

Revelation 13.1-10

It is often following the clearest vision of triumph that so many people go through the greatest severity of testing. We see this in Jesus' desert experience directly after his baptism, and we can see the same pattern here, too.

Having depicted the absolute nature of the victory won in the heavenly realms in the previous chapter, John now shows us the stark reality of conflict and pressure in the earthly sphere. The forces of empire, inspired and empowered by the defeated dragon, make all the claims that rightly belong to God alone – matchless power, amazing resilience, commanding authority. And, as the empire makes these claims, so it attacks and appears to conquer God's people. As the empire claims to be the only source of true peace and lasting prosperity, it demands absolute loyalty to its values and will tolerate no dissent.

This stark contrast has been clear since the beginning. John opens his letter by introducing himself as 'your brother in kingdom, suffering and patient endurance' (1.9). If we want to live in kingdom victory, we need to be ready for kingdom suffering, because kingdom living will continually bring us into conflict with the empires of this world. But God's gift to us – and to our suffering brothers and sisters – is the patient endurance that is borne in the knowledge that, though suffering comes, the end is secure.

COLLECT

Heavenly Father,
whose blessed Son was revealed
 to destroy the works of the devil
and to make us the children of God and heirs of eternal life:
grant that we, having this hope,
may purify ourselves even as he is pure;
that when he shall appear in power and great glory
we may be made like him in his eternal and glorious kingdom;
where he is alive and reigns with you,
in the unity of the Holy Spirit,
one God, now and for ever.

Ordinary Time: All Saints to Advent

Psalms **78.1-39** *or* 120, **121**, 122
Daniel 12
Revelation 13.11-end

Saturday 22 November

Revelation 13.11-end

'Everyone has their price' – maybe or maybe not, but everyone has their number. At least they did in the first century, before a separate number system was invented. Every letter had a numerical value, and so you could work out the value of every word and name by adding up the value of the letters in it. It isn't difficult to work out the number of your own name, once you know how the numbers are assigned.

So, it would not have been difficult for John's readers to make sense of the numbers in verse 18. They could work out fairly easily that the number of 'the beast' is 666 (though a later scribe noted that the number of 'of the beast' is in fact 616, hence the variant readings) – just as the number of the 'angel' in chapter 22 is 144. Neither would it have been difficult for them to work out that the number of 'Neron Caesar' (as his name was sometimes spelled) was also 666. If you want to know what the empire is really about, simply look at its most notorious emperor.

John isn't inviting us to clever calculations or cryptic codings, but to have 'wisdom' – spiritual insight concerning the world about us. Are we alert to the forces in our world that are making claims of empire? Who or what is claiming to be the real source of rest and contentment, of purpose and prosperity around us? And, having identified these claims, are we ready to stand against them and to call people to the true source of satisfaction and salvation?

> Heavenly Lord,
> you long for the world's salvation:
> stir us from apathy,
> restrain us from excess
> and revive in us new hope
> that all creation will one day be healed
> in Jesus Christ our Lord.

COLLECT

Ordinary Time: All Saints to Advent

Monday 24 November

Psalms 92, **96** *or* 123, 124, 125, **126**
Isaiah 40.1-11
Revelation 14.1-13

Revelation 14.1-13

After the distinct visions of the previous two chapters, the text tumbles into ever greater complexity. Images from earlier – of a voice from heaven, of worship, of the Lamb and of the 144,000 – mingle together with the anticipation of events to come, such as the first mention of the fall of Babylon. This kaleidoscope is both perplexing and inspiring – this is where we find the 'traditional' notion of sitting on clouds playing harps, just as 'pearly gates' come from chapter 21.

The complexity reminds us that there are issues here, about election and promise, judgement and holiness, that stretch language to its limits and beyond. The 144,000 are male, as they have 'not defiled themselves with women'. But they are also 'virgins', the usual female word. Just as this carefully numbered group are in fact without number (7.4, 9) so the symbolism of sexual purity stands for something much larger – faithful witness after the pattern of their Lord.

We are reminded that this group is merely the 'first fruits' (v.4) of a much larger harvest. While the text may appear to revel in judgement and condemnation, as elsewhere in Revelation there is a constant undercurrent of the possibility of repentance for those of 'every nation and tribe and language and people' from which this group is drawn. There are moments when we need to stop rationalizing these paradoxes of faith, and simply live them out.

COLLECT

Eternal Father,
whose Son Jesus Christ ascended to the throne of heaven
    that he might rule over all things as Lord and King:
keep the Church in the unity of the Spirit
and in the bond of peace,
and bring the whole created order to worship at his feet;
who is alive and reigns with you,
in the unity of the Holy Spirit,
one God, now and for ever.

Ordinary Time: All Saints to Advent

Psalms **97**, 98, 100 *or* **132**, 133
Isaiah 40.12-26
Revelation 14.14 – end of 15

Tuesday 25 November

Revelation 14.14 – end of 15

'Why do today what you can put off until tomorrow?' This appealing saying embodies that all-too-human ambivalence about judgement. Deadlines and financial crises, essay marks and competition results all share that quality of judgement. They are designed to set standards, to show what is important and of value, and distinguish it from what is not. In our tolerant age, it isn't socially acceptable to render judgement about anything or anyone. And yet, without it, we never know what is really of value and can all too easily sink into a sea of mediocrity.

That said, this passage reminds us that our own evaluations are always partial and ultimately inadequate. By repeating the word 'sickle' seven times, John is telling us that there is only one who has the right to render complete judgement – and that he will do so. That judgement, moreover, is always surprising and cuts across human boundaries. Just as the Song of Moses, first given to one nation, has been taken up by those from many nations, so they, in turn, invite all nations to accept the call to holy living and to welcome the costly grace that has already overflowed to them.

An increasing number of subcultures in our land are untouched by the good news of what God has done in Christ. We must sing the Song of Moses in a key they will understand, if they are to be prepared for the judgement that is to come.

> God the Father,
> help us to hear the call of Christ the King
> and to follow in his service,
> whose kingdom has no end;
> for he reigns with you and the Holy Spirit,
> one God, one glory.

COLLECT

Ordinary Time: All Saints to Advent

Wednesday 26 November

Psalms 110, 111, **112**
or **119.153-end**
Isaiah 40.27 – 41.7
Revelation 16.1-11

Revelation 16.1-11

As Revelation unfolds, we return to the series of sevenfold judgements that depict the way the world is and God's response. Earlier, in the seals of chapter 6 and the trumpets of chapter 8, the subjects of the judgements appeared to be humanity in general, though with God's people protected. Now that we have seen more clearly the spiritual battle between the one on the throne and the dragon and his allies, the nature of the judgements has a sharper focus. The fifth bowl is poured out 'on the throne of the beast' (v.10), that is, on the very place that has set itself against God's authority over his world.

Now the judgements are depicted specifically as a re-enactment of the plagues against Egypt in the first Exodus. Reflecting on these, we are faced with the same challenges as those presented by that first instance – weighty questions such as the nature of God's sovereignty, the justice of judgement, the place of compassion. In the midst of this, we are also presented with two kinds of suffering. There is suffering that arises from rebellion against God, which calls for repentance lest it end in judgement. And there is the suffering of the people of God as a result of the faithful witness, which calls for patient endurance and will end in vindication.

COLLECT

Eternal Father,
whose Son Jesus Christ ascended to the throne of heaven
    that he might rule over all things as Lord and King:
keep the Church in the unity of the Spirit
and in the bond of peace,
and bring the whole created order to worship at his feet;
who is alive and reigns with you,
in the unity of the Holy Spirit,
one God, now and for ever.

Ordinary Time: All Saints to Advent

Psalms **125**, 126, 127, 128
or **143**, 146
Isaiah 41.8-20
Revelation 16.12-end

Thursday 27 November

Revelation 16.12-end

This series of judgements now reaches its climax, as those who have set themselves against God line up for the final conflict. The central figures here remain the dragon and its henchmen, the beast from the sea and the beast from the land, now seen clearly as the false prophet. False claims to power go hand in hand with false claims to worship.

This third picture of the end complements the previous two. Where there will be silence and prayer (8.1), celebration and worship (11.15), there will also be destruction and retribution. Judgement brings both affirmation of what is good and negation of what is bad. God is redeeming his people but also destroying those who destroy (11.18) if they will not turn from the path of destruction.

The sudden interjection in v.15, recalling the teaching of both Jesus (Matthew 25) and Paul (1 Thessalonians 5), reminds us that cosmic judgement always has a personal element and personal consequences. We, too, living in the light of future judgement, need to say 'yes' to the good and 'no' to the bad in our lives if we are to be appropriately dressed for the world that is to come.

God the Father,
help us to hear the call of Christ the King
and to follow in his service,
whose kingdom has no end;
for he reigns with you and the Holy Spirit,
one God, one glory.

COLLECT

Ordinary Time: All Saints to Advent

Friday 28 November

Psalms **139** *or* 142, **144**
Isaiah 41.21 – 42.9
Revelation 17

Revelation 17

After the twists and turns of the last chapters, we now turn a corner at the start of this chapter and enter the long finishing straight to the climax of the book. John is promised a vision of judgement, but he is 'amazed with a great amazement' (v.6) because he sees a vision of splendour and opulence that looks anything but temporary.

But once again, as in 13.18, there is the call for understanding and wisdom, *nous* and *sophia* (v.9). And again, this is not a puzzle to be decoded so that we can work out which king is which and pin down the date when Revelation was written – John's readers do not need to know which emperor is reigning! Rather, they need to understand the significance of this reign, and the empire's claims to *pax*, *victoria* and *aeterna*. This empire wars against itself (v.16); its strength evaporates in the face of the one who was slain but is now alive for evermore (v.14); and, impressive though it is, its kings will reign for a mere hour (v.12).

Having discerned, following chapter 13, which forces in our world are now making claims of empire, we now need to discern the real nature of these claims in the light of the one who is to come. 'All my hope on God is founded' says the hymn, for every other 'tower and temple fall to dust.'

COLLECT

Eternal Father,
whose Son Jesus Christ ascended to the throne of heaven
  that he might rule over all things as Lord and King:
keep the Church in the unity of the Spirit
and in the bond of peace,
and bring the whole created order to worship at his feet;
who is alive and reigns with you,
in the unity of the Holy Spirit,
one God, now and for ever.

Ordinary Time: All Saints to Advent

Psalms **145** *or* **147**
Isaiah 42.10-17
Revelation 18

Saturday 29 November

Revelation 18

Now, at last, we see the 'towers and temples' collapse in slow motion. The destruction is as sudden as it is unexpected; all Babylon's strength and wealth are gone in 'one hour' (vv.10,17,19). And, in the destruction, her true nature is revealed.

The sexual imagery of chapter 17 is now displaced by images of wealth and luxury; the 'fornication' has been the idolizing of the pursuit of wealth. Just as the worship of the beast involves total economic control (13.17), so here the list of 28 (4 x 7) cargoes (vv.12–13) symbolizes complete control of the resources of every corner of the earth. The destructive and dehumanizing nature of this quest is made clear; the climax of the list is the trade of human lives.

This rejoicing in judgement is no mere triumphalism. For it is a judgement of hope. Seven times we meet the 'kings of the earth' who, though rightly ruled by Christ, have worshipped the beast, and so are subject to its judgement. But then we meet them an eighth time, as those who 'bring their glory' into the New Jerusalem (21.24); mercy has triumphed over judgement. And it is a judgement of liberation; God's decisive declaration (v.20) is for the oppressed people of God against those who have been oppressing them.

As always, it calls for personal response. How can we, living in our empire, 'come out of her' (v.4) and live in the world but not of it (John 17.15)?

COLLECT

God the Father,
help us to hear the call of Christ the King
and to follow in his service,
whose kingdom has no end;
for he reigns with you and the Holy Spirit,
one God, one glory.

**Book 5
Reflections for
Daily Prayer:
Advent –
2 before Lent**

Publication date:
October 2008

Contributors:
Alan Garrow
Susan Hope
Keith Ward
Bruce Gillingham
Sarah Dylan Breuer
Stephen Croft

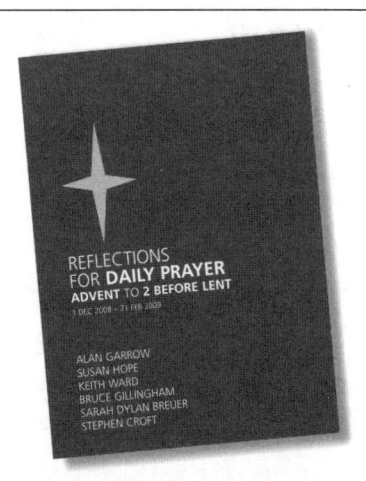

£3.99 978 0 7151 4160 1

Reflections for Daily Prayer is published four times a year – October, January, April and July – and is available from all good Christian bookshops. You can also obtain it direct from the publishers (see below).

Subscribe today

For more information on the *Reflections* series, ordering and subscriptions, visit **www.dailyprayer.org.uk**

Annual UK subscription for four editions	£17.50
Europe	£19.00
Rest of world	£21.50

(all include postage and packing)

It is also possible to arrange gift subscriptions.

Prices correct at time of going to press.